"A book for everyone who has ever felt like a 'fake Christian.' Solid and credible—filled with laughter and tears coming from the heart of a woman on her journey to mature faith. It's a keeper!"

—**Carol Kent,** speaker,
author of *When I Lay My Isaac Down*

"Connie Cavanaugh gives you insights…as she walks alongside you like a trusted friend. God pursues us even in the wilderness, and I believe He has given Connie this message as part of His pursuit of us."

—**Bob Reccord,**
President, North American Mission Board,
Southern Baptist Convention; coauthor of
Made to Count and *Strike Zone*

"Honesty, vulnerability, confession, and brokenness are exactly what the Lord asks of us, and Connie is giving us permission to experience all four…Thank you, Connie, for revealing the truth…with gentleness, scripture, and humor!"

—**Karen Covell,** TV producer,
author of *How to Talk About Jesus Without Freaking Out*

"Sometimes a book hits a spiritual nerve. This one struck mine… Practical theology that, if actually practiced, would result in authentic and liberating Christ-filled living."

—**Margaret Gibb,**
President, Women Alive, Canada

"If doubts from unanswered prayers or life's disappointments cause you to wander, this book is a compass that will help lead you back to an authentic relationship with a loving God."

—**Randy Singer,** award-winning author of
Directed Verdict and *Self Incrimination*

෴෴෴

"Connie's...insights into the human spirit will stretch you, amuse you, and—ultimately—challenge you to grow. Don't miss this book!"

—**Carolyn Curtis,** author; contributing editor
to *OnMission* magazine

෴෴෴

"Connie is a masterful storyteller. The stories she tells are about us and where we live. *From Faking It to Finding Grace* will move you, convict you, and encourage and bless you. I urge you to read this profoundly relevant and life-changing book."

—**Richard Blackaby,** president, Canadian
Southern Baptist Seminary; coauthor of
Experiencing God Day by Day and *Spiritual Leadership*

From Faking It
to
Finding Grace

CONNIE CAVANAUGH

HARVEST HOUSE PUBLISHERS

EUGENE, OREGON

Unless otherwise indicated, all Scripture quotations are taken from the Holman Christian Standard Bible®, Copyright © 1999, 2000, 2002, 2003 by Holman Bible Publishers. Used by permission. Holman Christian Standard Bible®, Holman CSB®, and HCSB® are federally registered trademarks of Holman Bible Publishers.

Verses marked NIV are taken from the HOLY BIBLE, NEW INTERNATIONAL VERSION®. NIV®. Copyright©1973, 1978, 1984 by the International Bible Society. Used by permission of Zondervan. All rights reserved.

Verses marked NCV are taken from *The Holy Bible, New Century Version,* Copyright © 1987, 1988, 1991 by Word Publishing, Nashville, TN 37214. Used by permission.

Verses marked MSG are taken from The Message. Copyright © by Eugene H. Peterson 1993, 1994, 1995, 1996, 2000, 2001, 2002. Used by permission of NavPress Publishing Group.

Verses marked NASB are taken from the New American Standard Bible®, © 1960, 1962, 1963, 1968, 1971, 1972, 1973, 1975, 1977, 1995 by The Lockman Foundation. Used by permission. (www.Lockman.org)

Verses marked KJV are taken from the King James Version of the Bible.

Verses marked NKJV are taken from the New King James Version. Copyright ©1982 by Thomas Nelson, Inc. Used by permission. All rights reserved.

All brackets in quotations from the Holman Christian Standard Bible are in the orginal.

The Scripture verses on page 229 are taken from the NKJV.

Cover by Garborg Design Works, Minneapolis, Minnesota

Cover images © Jules Frazier/Photodisc Green/Getty Images; F Schussler/PhotoLink/Photodisc Green/Getty Images

FROM FAKING IT TO FINDING GRACE

Copyright © 2005 by Connie Cavanaugh
Published by Harvest House Publishers
Eugene, Oregon 97402
www.harvesthousepublishers.com

Library of Congress Cataloging-in-Publication Data
Cavanaugh, Connie, 1955-
  From faking it to finding grace / Connie Cavanaugh.
    p. cm.
  ISBN-10: 0-7369-1528-1 (pbk.)
  ISBN-13: 978-0-7369-1528-1 (pbk.)
  1. Spiritual life—Christianity.   2. Hidden God.   I. Title.
  BV4501.3.C42 2005
  248.8'6—dc22   2005001505

Printed in the United States of America

08 09 10 11 12 13   / VP-MS /   10 9 8 7 6 5 4 3

My husband, Gerry, and my children—Christine and her husband,
Brad; Anita; and JP—paid the dearest price. Not only did they release
me, cover for me, and revive me with steaming tea,
they never stopped believing that this day would come.
This book belongs to them with all my heart.

Be merciful to those who doubt.

CONTENTS

CHAPTER ONE

The Road *More* Traveled

I deserted you for a brief moment,
but I will take you back with great compassion.
God speaking through the prophet Isaiah

Not all who wander are lost.
J.R.R. Tolkien, *The Fellowship of the Ring*

*P*alms sweating, heart thudding, I darted glances at the others in the room and quickly lowered my head. I had learned in elementary school that the best way to be overlooked was to avoid eye contact with the teacher. Forty years later it was still an effective tactic. I hid my discomfort behind a well-rehearsed "poker face."

There were only a dozen or so of us there, ostensibly all for the same reason. Only I knew different. I knew I was the only one there because I had to be. I was the only one who had no choice.

I waited, hoping against hope that someone else would take the bait and answer the question I couldn't answer—well, not truthfully anyway. No one did. So the pastor repeated the question with an encouraging smile. And waited.

"What has God been doing in your life this week?"

I began leafing through my Bible, pretending to look for that elusive scripture that had supposedly impacted me one day last week. If I could just locate that little gem, I would be happy to take the floor and tell everyone about the marvelous insights and life-changing tips I was daily gleaning from my personal devotions. It was a ruse, of course. There were no personal devotions. The last time I had opened my Bible was one week earlier—same time, same place, same reason.

Relief washed over me as a woman spoke up at last. The group sharing time where the pastor asked the inevitable what-has-God-been-doing question was done. Now I just had to join a talkative group of fervent pray-ers and let them do most of the work, and the toughest hour of my week would be over. I had survived another Wednesday-night prayer meeting with my secret still intact.

As I drove away from the church, it hit me once again how I had come full circle—from darkness to numbness with an exciting interlude in between. I felt hopeless and alone. *If only I could just walk away from religion and quietly lead a hermit's life of tending my flowers and decorating my home I would be so much happier,* I thought for the millionth time. But I knew that was impossible. I was a Sunday-school teacher. I played keyboard in the worship band. Church was a huge part of my life. Not only that, I was married to the church: My husband, once a pastor, was still in full-time ministry. I knew that in order for him to live out his call, I must be a supportive wife. If I didn't share his living faith, I needed to pretend, I thought.

Feeling Trapped

I kept coming back to the same thing: The only choice I had was no choice at all. Telling the truth was not possible. Because if I told the truth—*that I had once been a fervent believer but had somehow lost my faith and didn't know where to find it*—my husband's ministry would be over. If not over, then seriously hindered. The only way I could stop living a lie was to leave him and dissolve the marriage. That would kill his ministry even quicker! I loved my husband. I loved my family. Divorce was never an option. So I had to keep faking it, I thought. For my husband's sake. Once again, I felt hopeless and alone.

> It seems like we all know someone who is going through a season of dryness or doubt...but it's never us. No one ever admits to being there now.

I had been a Christian long enough to know that spiritual dryness is a taboo subject in the church. Nobody ever talks about it, except in the third person. It seems like we all know someone who is going through a season of dryness or doubt...but it's never us. No one ever admits to being there now. If people do admit to a season of dryness, it is almost always in the past and, happily, they're now cured. Close to God again. Whew!

The Road *More* Traveled

I had never read the writings of Augustine, Martin Luther, Teresa of Avila, John of the Cross, Thomas à Kempis, Thomas Aquinas, or more recently, Mother Teresa. Distracted by the demands of raising my family, I left that sort of reading to "professional Christians." Had I interrupted my busyness to do some study, I would have been surprised to discover that spiritual wilderness—a place of dry faith characterized by the inability to connect with a seemingly silent God—was not as rare as I had thought. It certainly was not unique to me. Rather, among the great writers, thinkers, and reformers of Christian history, it was, and is, the road *more* traveled. And it was not something to be dismissed as a detour in an otherwise well-spent life of faith. The wilderness experience provides the Christian a school for the soul where he can shed his unworkable childish faith and forge a mature faith, a faith that works in the real world. The wilderness helps us dismantle our false gods and discover the real God.

John of the Cross, who outlined his wilderness experience in *Dark Night of the Soul,* and his mentor Teresa of Avila (and her work *Interior Castle)* were unknown to me as I struggled with guilt and doubt. Had I known of heroes of the faith—or even fellow believers today—who had preceded me in wrestling with doubt, feelings of abandonment, and a seemingly unresponsive God, I may have taken some comfort and not drifted for so long.

As it was, I thought I was the only one. And I did everything I could to hide the truth and fake what I thought an authentic Christian life should look like. Mostly I lived with the unsettled feeling that I would slip up, expose the sham behind my mask, and reveal my hollow soul.

Those who have never spent any time in the wilderness are prone to think they are immune. We all know people like that. That's what I was like as a new believer when prayers were answered to my liking and blessings flowed from above. If someone had told me back then that ten years later I would be far out in the spiritual wilderness, I would have scoffed. Me? No way! My relationship with God was rock-solid, I claimed. Boy, was I in for a big surprise.

The Conspiracy of Silence

If spiritual dryness is swept under the pew, just imagine the pressure to sweep it under the pulpit. To think that deacons, pastors, elders, worship leaders, Bible-study teachers, or missionaries might be struggling with doubt...we can't even consider that. Believe it or not, in my travels as a conference speaker I have found that the majority of people who approach me—always in secret—to confess their struggle with dry faith are leaders in the church or people in full-time ministry. There is a conspiracy of silence that bars the topic of our current spiritual doubt from being publicly confessed.

When I discussed this topic with my friend Kathy, who has written and taught a Bible study for seekers and new believers, she noted a "funny observation. There was a period of time," she told me, "when several people confessed to me they doubted the existence of God and asked me what to do. They were all new Christians. Could it be they had not yet learned they were supposed to play the 'cover-up' game?" From my experience, her observation is accurate. As a new believer I was much more open and confessional about my real thoughts, including my doubts. As time passed, I grew more and more guarded as I perceived a subtle pressure to put such "childish things" behind me.

The truth is, almost every believer experiences periods of doubt or dry faith at some point in his or her life of faith, but she dare not admit it. Sadly, we keep our doubts hush-hush—and the wilderness wanderer feels alone at a time when he or she needs support more than ever. In the past 30 years, I cannot remember hearing more than once or twice a public request for prayer from someone who was suffering from debilitating doubt. This unbelief, if not addressed, has the potential to smother our relationship with God and our Christian peers and eventually drive doubters away from church. Some never return.

Who Is the "Wilderness Wanderer"?

The wanderer is a Christian who, at some point in life, has begun a faith journey by choosing to place his faith and trust in Jesus Christ. The wanderer, though a child of God, is not enjoying the fruits of that relationship. The wanderer no longer sees (or has yet to see) the work of God in his life or the lives of others. He doubts that God loves him or wants a relationship, as prayers seem to go unanswered or, he thinks, maybe even unheard. He is troubled and dismayed by the suffering all around him, suffering that a so-called loving God does nothing about.

The wanderer may doubt the existence of God and wonder if the life of faith he formerly experienced was all smoke and mirrors. If, like me, he stays active in church, he will fake an authentic relationship with Christ in order to hide the dryness. Some wanderers drop out of church, drifting further and further from God with the loss of Christian influence. Others drop in, arriving just in time or a bit late for the service. They find a getaway seat near the back or in the balcony and are out the door before the last "Amen" has sounded. This type of church attendance is akin to punching a time card at a factory. There is little chance that this "worshiper" will encounter God. The wanderer is restlessly in search of a peace and communion he once knew or has yet to discover. But at present peace eludes him at every turn.

Some wanderers lose hope, drop out of church, and refer to themselves as "former" believers—ex-Christians. I know of several people who once exhibited vibrant faith but who now eschew all practice of religion and claim to no longer believe. Other wanderers, who remain connected to the community of faith, can live for years in a spiritual wasteland, gorging on material or relational pursuits in the attempt to fill the vacuum a sense of His presence once occupied. They learn to wear masks at church and hide behind an outward appearance of "togetherness."

Letting the Cat out of the Bag

The first time I publicly confessed to being a wanderer was when I spoke to a group of about a hundred women in a neighboring province. (I will explain further how it was that I was a conference speaker at a time when my spirit was so dry.) Many of the women in the audience had known me for years. I didn't go too deeply into detail. I didn't dare, because at that point I had few answers to give and little advice to offer. I wasn't too sure how I had wound up in the wilderness in the first place, and I did not yet see a clear path leading out. I was simply being obedient to what I perceived to be the nudging of the Holy Spirit to tell the truth. The fact that I had "heard" any counsel from God at all in my wilderness condition was huge. While I could not offer a prescription for healing, I did tell the women I had hope—because even though I still felt spiritually estranged from God, I sensed I was at least facing in the right direction for the first time in years. I later learned that this simple act of obedience was a key step on the road to recovery.

After I delivered that first public confession, I felt ill. Not one person commented on that portion of my talk. They thanked me for the stories that made them laugh, but nobody said anything about what was uppermost in my mind. I couldn't wait to escape to the privacy of my room, where I planned to eat all the chocolate I could find and cry myself to sleep. Worst-case scenario: My husband would lose his job. Added to that, the person who had asked me to speak would want me to step down so she could find someone more suitable to take my place. To avoid that shame, I planned to tell her in the morning that I couldn't continue.

I returned to the motel, heartsick. As I plodded heavily up the outdoor staircase to my room, a woman softly called my name. In the darkness I couldn't see her. She had been waiting in the shadows. As we neared one another I recognized her. She had been invited to this event to lead a conference. She had been in full-time Christian service for several years. What she told me caught me completely by surprise.

"I've never heard any speaker talk about spiritual dryness before," she began. *(Well, you won't hear it from me again. I'm quitting in the morning!)* "I didn't really expect to get anything from this conference, because I came here to do my job and didn't think that God would speak to me," she continued, her voice beginning to waver. "The truth is, I have been feeling dry for a couple of years now. I haven't been able to figure out why it happened or how to fix it." Tears welled up in her eyes.

"I can certainly relate to that," I agreed.

"I just can't fake it any more. I'm so tired of living a double life. Actually, I had decided this would be my swan song. I was planning to resign when I got home." By now we were both teary-eyed. "I have felt so alone! I haven't been able to tell a soul for fear of losing my job. But what you said tonight gave me hope. Just knowing I'm not the only one. You don't know what that means!" she said, grasping my hand.

"Oh yes, I do!" I needed to hear her confession as badly as she had needed to hear mine.

"I know God brought me here for a reason," she continued. "I'm going to take this as a sign and I'm not going to quit."

"Me neither!" I decided.

Wanderers Need Hope

One of the biggest hindrances to finding help for dry faith is this behind-closed-doors mentality. That's why both I and the woman I met felt so alone. Until I finally came clean and publicly confessed I was a wanderer, I truly thought I was the only one out there. The thing a dry believer needs more than anything else is *hope*. That is the word I hear every single time someone identifies with my experience. They invariably say, "What you said gave me hope." Hope for what, you might ask?

- Hope that God really is who He says He is.

- Hope that if someone else has been a wanderer and has found a way out of the wilderness, maybe you can too.

- Hope that once again you will see His hand at work in and around your life.

- Hope that after such a long silence, you will hear His voice guiding, teaching, admonishing, comforting.

- Hope that the Bible can be trusted and can become a Living Word again.

- Hope that you will once again burn with the desire to share the good news because it *is* good news again!

- Hope that your restless spirit will be replaced with a deep sense of satisfaction, a peace that truly cannot be understood by the human mind.

- Hope for a relationship that transcends anything you can experience in the flesh.

One month later, I gave the same series of talks in another province and experienced the same reaction: public silence, private confession. Another woman came to me in secret. "I had not planned on coming here tonight," she began. "The only reason I came is because someone tricked me to get me in the door and once I was here, I didn't know how to escape without being noticed." She was the wife of a local pastor and was well-known.

"I don't know how it happened or why but I seem to have lost all interest in God. I feel like He is so distant. I never see Him or hear Him anymore." I told her that was exactly what had happened to me and that I was still a long way from having all the answers. I was just being obedient by telling the truth. "This has been really hard on my husband," she continued. "It's not too cool for a pastor to have a wife who doubts more than she believes!" Again, I could relate. "But something you said tonight gave me hope. For the first time in a long time, I sensed God's presence. Maybe it's not too late for me to get my faith back. Will you pray for me?"

"Will you do the same for me?" I asked.

There will be times, depending on how long you have been in the wilderness, when hope is nothing more than a faint glow on the horizon. Like the midday sun that barely peeks over the edge of the world in late-December Alaska, it brightens the sky just enough to convince you it's still there. That faint dawning says, *Don't lose hope!* What you see now as a dull shimmer for a short time each day will surely shine with great intensity, never setting on some days, *in another season*. Don't give up. Hang on! Things will get brighter.

Confession as the Gateway

I continued sharing my story every few weeks in different speaking venues and slowly awakened to the reality that there were many others in the wilderness as well. I discovered that many Christians go through dry times of varying duration and intensity during the course of their spiritual pilgrimage. God continued to work on me, calling me back into authentic fellowship with Him, teaching me, and encouraging me through the stories of other wanderers. For some, dry spells are sporadic—they come and go. They have short spans of feeling like God is silent or a small niggling of doubt that never takes a firm hold. For others, like me, a dry spell can last so long you begin to doubt everything. You even wonder if your conversion experience was real.

Because of the pressure, real or imagined, to keep silent about our doubts, wanderers endure in silence and either quietly drift away, never to return—or keep it to themselves and live a lie. The path that leads out of the wilderness is paved with truth: "Confess your sins to one another and pray for one another, so that you may be healed" (James 5:16). I desperately needed healing; I needed to be restored to life. It was not until I began to come out of hiding and confess the truth that God began watering my tinder-dry soul.

What Does a Wanderer Look Like?

On the surface wanderers look just like authentic Christians, but their hearts are vastly different. One is satisfied with Jesus, the other is never satisfied. One is thirsty for God, the other is just plain thirsty. The Holy Spirit guides one; the other is driven by self-centered pursuits. One is surrendered to His will; the other is crouching in a stance of self-protection. One is hopeful about the future; the other is bound by fear. However, in church on Sunday morning, we wear the same styles, sing the same songs, amen the same preachers, drop money in the same plates. "These people come near to me with their mouth and honor me with their lips, but their hearts are far from me" (Isaiah 29:13 NIV).

How do I know if I am a wanderer? Here are some questions that will clarify your thinking if you honestly answer them:

- Do you operate from a sense of duty (as opposed to a spirit of gratitude)?

- Have you lost (or never found) the desire to share the gospel with unbelievers?

- Do you have to feign enthusiasm when hearing that someone has chosen to follow Christ?

- Are you driven by material pursuits while paying lip service to God?

- Do you go to church to "get it over with" (rather than to encounter God)?

- Are you apathetic about matters of faith and spirituality, eager to change the topic when discussion arises?

- Do you pray, other than to "bless the food and the hands that made it"?

- Is your Bible more than a Sunday accessory?

- Do you ever feel like a hypocrite? Like you are leading a double life?

If you answered yes to some or all of these questions, your relationship with the living God has room for improvement. Growth is what this book is all about. Travel with me as we look at the wilderness experience as an opportunity to shed an unworkable, immature, underdeveloped faith and learn to forge a faith that works in the real world—where bad things happen to good people. You move out of the wilderness by moving toward the Father—*as He really is,* not as you have thought He was. You learn to recognize your false gods and begin to know and experience and believe the God of Scripture, who draws us to Himself with His pursuing love.

Will This Book Help Me?

If you have read this far, I assume you are at least curious about the topic of dry faith. Maybe you feel like you have a pretty good relationship with God but you are unsure about that whole area of "hearing His voice" and "seeing His hand." You are skeptical when others say things like "God told me to do this" or "God clearly spoke to me about that." *Why don't I ever see or hear Him like that?* you wonder. *Is it possible I'm missing something in my Christian experience?* You enjoy the worship hour at your church and attend a friendly Bible-study group, and most of your friends are at church—but you feel restless and want to go deeper.

Or perhaps you go to church only because it is politically expedient—a great place to make contacts for your business. You enjoy the pastor's messages as long as he doesn't get too personal or ask for money too often. The people at church are nice enough and you appreciate the values your children are learning in Sunday school. But you've noticed some people seem to have something you don't. It's not that you don't want what they have, it's that you're not sure if you're willing to pay the price.

Maybe you are someone who used to hear and see God at work in your life, but He's been quiet and out of sight for so long you've almost convinced yourself He's not real. You think you've been hoodwinked by clever religious propaganda and the joke is on you. You are desperate for some celestial sign. If God doesn't reveal Himself to you soon, you're going to walk away and never come back. Maybe some fervent believer has even taken you on as a project, vowing to make you see the God they so clearly encounter each day. But no matter what they say or how hard they pray, nothing changes. You feel spiritually dead…and so alone.

Or perhaps you are a believer who has always lacked spark and enthusiasm. You came to Christ at an early age and have never known the mountaintop or the valley. The only reason you read your Bible is because you know you should. You never miss church, and you even attend Bible studies and conferences, retreats and seminars, looking for the excitement you've heard talked about by vibrant Christian leaders and speakers. But it just hasn't happened to you. Your faith is, well, boring! It seems like nothing exciting ever happens in your life, and you haven't ever led someone to faith in Christ. You're not really lost in the wilderness—but you feel as though there must be something more.

∽∽∽

If the faith you've had up until now has not stood the test of real life, it is underdeveloped. It is immature. The faith I had in my early years as a believer was a black-and-white, Jesus-is-the-answer faith. While Jesus truly is the answer, I no longer claim to have the inside track on His will or His ways. A mature faith realizes that there are large areas of gray that we will never understand until we see Him face-to-face. Mature faith stays the course when shattered dreams, unfulfilled desires, or unthinkable tragedy attempts to derail our life. Mature faith says, like Job who had lost everything including his health, his children, and the esteem of his friends and family, "Though He slay me, I will hope in Him" (Job 13:15 NASB). What is our goal? Mature faith in the real God.

Jesus says, "Blessed are those who hunger and thirst for righteousness, for they will be filled" (Matthew 5:6 NIV). Righteousness is right relationship. If we long for a right relationship with God, He will make it happen. Anytime we feel dry or are plagued by doubt, He desires so much more for us. Our dark night can be a school for the soul—it can drive us to a mature relationship with the Father. Our soul-hunger, a sense of longing for something more, is the first step in the right direction. Are you hungry?

Part One

The Dark Night:
A School for the Soul

CHAPTER TWO

Spiritual Drift

My God, my God, why have You forsaken me?
[Why are You] so far from my deliverance
and from my words of groaning?
King David

Where have you hidden, Beloved, and left me groaning?
St. John of the Cross

*A*manda was not afraid of challenge. She seldom looked for the easy road but rather determined to follow God's leading regardless of where it might take her. When she moved to a community for her first teaching job, she joined a small church and began cheerfully using her gifts there. She taught Sunday school, played piano, organized Vacation Bible School, and more. There were not many eligible bachelors in that church. But Amanda wasn't looking for a husband; she was trying to make a difference.

A couple of years into her tenure, a local family's eldest son returned from his world travels. For years Amanda had prayed, trusting that God would send her the man she was to spend the rest of her life with. When Brent dropped out of the sky and began to pursue her, Amanda was smitten. What could be more alluring than the tall, tanned adventurer who enthralled everyone with his stories? Within a year they were married. She could not have been happier.

The newlyweds moved to a large city, where Amanda taught school and Brent enrolled in college. Because of their age, they decided to start their family right away. Their first child, a healthy baby girl, brought renewed vigor to a marriage that had lost its initial luster. Two years later, their world was soundly rocked when their second baby was born with multiple serious handicaps. If she survived at all, she would need full-time care, require many surgeries, and never develop mentally beyond infancy. Amanda barely had time to absorb this devastating shock when Brent moved in with a classmate. A woman. He told his wife he had never loved her but had married her to please his parents. She was shattered.

Needing some distance from her husband's new living arrangement but unable to manage on her own with two preschoolers, one severely handicapped, Amanda returned to the town where she and Brent had met. She couldn't get her former teaching job back, so for the first year, she worked as a special-education assistant, a job that did not pay well. She had to rely on social assistance to make up the difference so she could afford day care.

Amanda reconnected with her old church but had little time for ministry. Trying to get two toddlers ready for church on Sunday morning meant she was almost always late. One Sunday, by the time she finally got the girls muscled into their winter gear and strapped into their car seats, it was already past starting time. Not ready to admit defeat, she still hoped to catch part of the service; worship times were like blood transfusions to her soul, giving her the strength to forge ahead. Climbing in the driver's side door, she landed with a thud on her block-of-ice seat. It was minus 30 outside and she had forgotten to "preheat" her car. She started the engine and then tried to close the door of her ancient Toyota; it shrieked in protest, resisting her heartiest tugs.

"God, please help!" she cried audibly, fighting the tears that were her constant companion. Grabbing the handle with both hands, she yanked hard, hoping to slam the door shut and block the Arctic blast. Clang! It ripped off its hinges, which were brittle with cold, and landed on the driveway with a clatter. Seeing the door lying there beside the car, the total absurdity of the situation brought forth a snort that was as close to a laugh as she'd gotten for a long while. Her response surprised her, but it was more welcome than tears. Still chuckling under her scarf, she unloaded the girls and lugged them back inside.

"I don't pray much anymore," Amanda reported when she told me this story later. I remember being startled and impressed by her courageous honesty. I got the sense from our conversation that she wasn't bitter or mad at God—she was just worn down emotionally and exhausted physically. She felt abandoned by Him, as well as her husband. In her words, "God seemed silent, sometimes for long periods. Things seemed so hopeless, so difficult, it was hard to go on." The God she had prayed to and trusted to provide for her seemed to have fallen down on the job.

Amanda's wilderness season illustrates a common difficulty for wanderers—they stop praying with faith and simply call out to God in desperation, hoping He'll hear and answer in some recognizable way. Some stop praying altogether. Amanda was not one of these, however. Although her prayers seemed ineffectual, she persevered.

She went back to the university at night, eventually getting her graduate diploma in special education. God rebuilt her life, giving her a new career and a new husband who loved her and her children, and renewed her faith. Fifteen years later, Amanda is a resource teacher in a school that has a high percentage of special-needs students. She comments, "I would have preferred to teach at my old job but I couldn't get into the regular system. God had plans there I couldn't see, but all those experiences have been valuable assets for what I do now."

The Pattern of Drift

Spiritual drift can be triggered by tragedy, or it can sneak up slowly, the result of many little irritations and wounds. That's how it was for me. Within a year of my conversion to Christianity as an 18-year-old college student, I was baptized. I threw myself into the life of the church, soaking it up like a dry sponge. Before long, I felt called to dedicate my life to serving God. The way I interpreted that call was to assume I would marry a preacher. So I went looking for one.

Fortunately, someone who fit the bill was also looking for me! Before long I married Gerry, a new believer and already a pastor. We rode off into the sunset, brought entire villages to faith in Christ, and lived happily ever after...

Well, that was the romanticized version that swam in my head back when. The real story is that, full of hope and promise, we began our married life in a northern village ministering to First Nations People, known as Canadian Indians at that time. And everywhere I went, I talked about my life transformed through the power of a living Savior, Jesus Christ. I saw many people believe and accept Christ's offer of grace and eternal life just like I had. This continued for many years. Nothing prepared me for the spiritual drift I was headed for.

I'm not sure when my journey into the wilderness of dry faith began. Like Amanda, I experienced surprises, disappointments, and what I perceived as unanswered prayers that eroded my trust in the God I knew at that time. I began to doubt He was really in charge and if He was, I wasn't sure I still wanted to go along for the ride. I started to protect myself from Him because, frankly, He was scaring me. The more I withdrew, the further we grew apart. As I look back now a pattern emerges, one I see in the lives of many wanderers:

1. In the early days of faith bad habits are broken, new friends are made, prayers are answered, and God seems near.

2. Life's natural disappointments—and God's failure to answer our prayers the way we expect—catch us by surprise, wound us, and wear us down emotionally and spiritually.

3. Our view of God changes, and we begin to be afraid of Him because He is not "protecting" us from life's pain.

4. We try to protect ourselves from further pain by subtly reasserting control over more and more of our life.

5. This wounded, fearful, self-protecting believer feels increasingly disconnected from God.

6. We call out to Him in frustration but get no recognizable response. We no longer sense His presence, hear His voice, or see His activity because the wall we have erected to keep pain out keeps God out too.

7. Losing hope and feeling forsaken, we grow cynical, put on a mask, and live the double life of a religious hypocrite imprisoned by the conspiracy of silence.

Deirdre's Drift

Deirdre has wonderful memories of growing up as a pastor's daughter. She married young and, along with her husband, who also became a pastor, roared into a future filled with promise. All during the years of raising four children, Deirdre developed and ran the children's program in their growing church. She loved being a pastor's wife. She enjoyed being a mom. She found fulfillment in her church involvement. Life was good for about 15 years.

Then she was blindsided by a series of shocks over a span of eight years. The first came from the unlikeliest corner. Her husband, a powerful leader and the "strong one" in the relationship, was sidelined with clinical depression. He took a six-month leave of absence from the church. For a while, they did not know if he would ever return to the pulpit. Then, her older daughter began to pull away and rebel against her parents' authority. Because Deirdre had been a compliant child, her daughter's sudden transformation and surly independence shocked her. Like the tremors of an earthquake, the crises moved outward from the epicenter of her marriage, to her family, to her church. A trusted family friend and church leader left in disgrace after a moral failure, deeply wounding the remaining pastoral staff. By that time, Deirdre's husband was back in the pastorate, and she worried that this latest tragedy would be a setback for him.

Not much later, her husband accepted a new job that required a long-distance move. In a different city and no longer a pastor's wife, Deirdre struggled to find her role. She became involved in children's programming in her new church because that's what she'd always enjoyed. But there was no joy in it; each week was a trial and a burden. Then came more aftershocks. Her older son, who was living on his own, called home one night in tears and confessed that his fiancée was pregnant. Her younger son fell in with the wrong crowd and dropped out of school. Her younger daughter missed her friends "back home," was miserable in their new city, and begged to return to her old chums.

This seemingly endless onslaught began to take its toll. Deirdre's faith faltered and grew weak. Her health began to suffer from the stress. Feeling guilty and heartsick, she resigned some of her church positions. By this time, her Bible reading was sporadic; she preferred the daily crossword in the newspaper. She didn't know why her faith no longer satisfied or why she felt so adrift. She wondered why God seemed so distant and why He had allowed her to suffer without sending His comforting presence. If ever she needed to see Him and to feel His presence, it was now. But He was invisible and silent. So many of her prayers went unanswered that although she did not stop praying, she doubted praying was having any effect.

> We pull in, trying to avoid further pain,
> attempting to "save" ourselves. But in the process,
> we temporarily lose our true connection with real life.

In the midst of all the disappointment, she kept quiet about her waning faith. She suffered in silence, thinking it was all her fault. If only she had more faith, she could handle these Job-like experiences, she thought. As the months wore on and she grew more discouraged, Deirdre never told anyone about her dark night of the soul other than her husband. Nonetheless, one by one, many of the circumstances that had been personally painful began to improve. Her older daughter was now happily married and active in her church, and their relationship had never been better. Her older son and his new wife had two beautiful babies and were also walking with the Lord. Being a grandmother was a brand-new area of fulfillment—a serendipitous gift. Her younger son was doing well in a sales career, and her younger daughter had made new friends at church and was a stellar student. Deirdre's husband had fully recovered and was using his experiences to help other pastors avoid burnout.

But she still felt dry.

Then Deirdre heard my "wilderness confession," and something I said connected with her in a kooky way. When I mentioned that my daily Bible reading had been replaced with the daily-newspaper crossword, she came to me in tears. "I'm where you are," she whispered. This was the first time she had admitted to someone outside her family that she was floundering in her faith.

We talked about her experience. When she had encountered unforeseen problems in her family and church that hurt and disappointed her, it caught her off guard. Why would troubles like this arise when she was devoting herself to the service of God and others? Wasn't God supposed to take care of her and her family? Unanswered questions chipped away at her confidence in God's provision. She doubted whether God really was in control. And if He *was* in control, she wasn't sure she liked the direction He was taking her. She did not know if she could trust Him. She began to be afraid of Him.

Without realizing it on a conscious level, both Deirdre and I reacted to life's disappointments by trying to protect ourselves from a God who seemed capricious and untrustworthy. We pulled in, trying to avoid further pain, attempting to "save" ourselves. But in the process, we temporarily lost our true connection with real life, "for whoever wants to save his life will lose it, but whoever loses his life because of Me will save it" (Luke 9:24). Larry Crabb, in *Shattered Dreams,* so aptly describes what we did, calling it the "first commandment of fallen thinking: *Trust no one and you shall live.*" He explains further, "It's hard enough to develop a personal relationship with an *invisible* God, one whose voice I never hear the way I hear a friend's voice over the phone; it's even harder to feel close to an *unresponsive* God."[1]

Drift Begins with Fear...

We all make millions of small choices every day. *Will I have toast or cereal? Will I wear the blue dress or the red skirt? The black tie or the golf shirt? Pumps or sandals?* We also regularly make choices that have greater consequences. *Do I accept this job offer that requires a move? Do I return to school for another degree? Do I ask for a raise? Do I buy that house? Can I trust God to provide for my needs, big and small, or not?*

Sometimes—and this is important—our choices are not mindful but are simply a reaction to our circumstances. Consider this scenario: If a co-worker makes negative comments about my performance as she gossips about me to other co-workers, it will hurt my feelings. In the future I will try to steer clear of that person so as to protect my fragile ego. My reaction, brought on by hurt, will affect all my future dealings with this individual. If she throws a party, I'll find an excuse to miss it. If she pops in to my office, I'll probably cut short the visit by claiming I have a lot of work to do that day. Before long, we may not cross paths at all, since it will be obvious it's a one-sided relationship. Now realize this—I may not even be aware I am avoiding this co-worker, since I am simply reacting to what I perceive to be a danger or a threat of further pain if I allow myself to get close to her. But over time, as I protect myself from possible pain and avoid the relationship, what might have been a friendship eventually fizzles out, and the best that can remain is a "professional" association between two people who happen to work for the same company. I am safe. But I am also alone.

Each one of these reactions—changes made in order to protect ourselves from perceived danger—might alter our life course by only a small degree. But as any sailor knows, when you are afloat on the vastness of the ocean, even an error of one degree can cause you to miss your landfall. Several of these "course alterations" can accumulate and result in disaster, causing the sailor to drift aimlessly on the seas for much longer than anticipated.

This is a picture of what happened to Deirdre and to me. Like Deirdre, I too had been wounded and disappointed by life and had begun to rely on myself instead of relying on God. A fearful reaction to the pain of life nudged each of us to protect ourselves from further pain. We didn't make a conscious decision to stop trusting God, but we began to be afraid of Him.

C.S. Lewis pointedly describes what the wounded wanderer does in the attempt to protect himself or herself from further pain:

> To love at all is to be vulnerable. Love anything, and your heart will certainly be wrung and possibly be broken. If you want to make sure of keeping it intact, you must give your heart to no one…Wrap it carefully round with hobbies and little luxuries; avoid all entanglements; lock it up safe in the casket or coffin of your selfishness. But in that casket—safe, dark, motionless, airless—it will change. It will not be broken; it will become unbreakable.[2]

The spiritual "drifter" edges away from the God who has failed to prevent pain thus far, protecting his heart by withholding it. Safe in the "coffin," it grows hard, maybe cynical—and with the passing of time, impenetrable and possibly irredeemable.[3]

There's something I call "Santa-god theology": If we are good little girls and boys, Santa-god will reward us with everything on our want list. But the painful realities of life in the real world don't support this belief. The wilderness school for the soul teaches us that God will not always protect us from suffering and disappointment. No—in fact, God may wish that we experience suffering and pain so that we come to know Him fully. Most immature people, like I was for too long, don't want to hear that.

...and Continues with Disobedience

Jesus' story of the two foundations is a good illustration of the wilderness process. In this account the houses are identical and so are the storms. The only differences in the story are the foundations and the men who built on them:

> Everyone who hears these words of Mine and acts on them will be like a sensible man who built his house on the rock. The rain fell, the rivers rose, and the winds blew and pounded that house. Yet it didn't collapse, because its foundation was on the rock. But everyone who hears these words of Mine and doesn't act on them will be like a foolish man who built his house on the sand. The rain fell, the rivers rose, the winds blew and pounded that house, and it collapsed. And its collapse was great! (Matthew 7:24-27).

Where some believers run into trouble and begin to drift is that we are caught off guard by the storms, even though Jesus warns us that storms *will* come. In the parable, the storms that assail both houses are exactly the same—*rain fell, rivers rose, winds blew and pounded the house*—but their effect is different. Why does one house survive? Because one man built his foundation on the rock.

And what is that rock? "Everyone who hears these words of Mine and acts on them will be like a sensible man who built his house on the rock." Hearing and acting on the words of Jesus is the rock-solid basis for faith. In other words, a relationship with a living God is absolutely necessary if one wants to "hear" what He has to say and then "act" on it.

Jesus' story is not about an old Christian and a young Christian. It's not about a smart Christian and a dumb one. It is about a believer who has an interactive relationship with a personal God (the one "who hears these words of Mine") and one who does not. It is about obedience ("and acts on them"). Every time we react in fear to the storms of life—pull in and try to protect ourselves—our crouching stance pictures our lack of trust in God. We are saying *no*. We think we are saying *I can't,* but we are really saying *I won't*. We are refusing to trust. "Everyone who hears these words of Mine and doesn't act on them will be like a foolish man who built his house on the sand." Each time we do this, we build on sand and we drift. In hindsight the wilderness process is not that complicated to understand. It is constructed of a series of little no's. The reason the wilderness seems so hard to figure out while the wanderer is in it is because many of the "no's" are not audible. They are simply reactions to the storms of life. They are attempts to protect oneself from further pain.

The Easier Road

Not everyone drifts into the wilderness as a result of disappointment or personal loss. Ray Stedman suggests that millions of believers drift into a lifestyle of hypocrisy because it is the easier road. Rather than living in transparent honesty before God—whereby the believer continually repents of sin and returns to the Father for forgiveness and restoration—"it is possible to avoid the pain and humiliation of these cycles of repentance and renewal by maintaining an outward façade of spiritual commitment, moral impeccability, and orthodox behavior," writes Stedman.[4] Such believers—wanderers according to my definition—give the appearance of spiritual maturity. Because they have learned the lingo and practiced all the steps to the evangelical jive, they look and sound like everybody else under the steeple. Inwardly, though, wanderers suspect their Christian life is a hollow shell, a "whitewashed tomb" (Matthew 23:27).

I clearly remember having that type of thinking invade my perspective as my husband and I and our children traveled to our new home in California in 1983. I had been a pastor's wife for five years at that point, and along with the thrill of seeing many people become followers of Christ, there had been much sadness as well. We had seen people get swallowed up in sin. We had seen death; we had seen entire families destroyed by poor choices. "Real life" had left a deep impression on my young heart and mind. It scared me. It left me feeling inadequate and afraid. I was emotionally exhausted and worried about the future.

I recall thinking, as we drove on to the campus of the seminary where my husband would study for the next four years, *I've been a pastor's wife for five years and I'm tired. I'm going to watch what other women on campus plan to do when they become pastors' wives. Maybe I've been doing too much.* That tiny thought, seemingly innocent, became a course alteration that kept me out at sea for a very long time. Whereas I began my life of faith with an attitude of "Here am I. Send me!"—after a few too many blows to the heart, I exhibited a new attitude: *Here am I. Spare me. Send someone else!*

Ray Stedman laments the fact that this external Christian lifestyle (the lifestyle I went looking for in order to protect myself from further heart pain like I experienced in my early years of faith) is so prevalent in North America today that many new believers, who do not have the ability to discern, don't even know there is anything wrong with it. A new Christian "drifts into it with only an occasional twinge of doubt or a rare, faint pang of conscience."[5] If you sense this is closer to your experience than the other examples given here, read on. The message is the same for all of us. Regardless of how we got there, we all want to find our way out of the wilderness.

Are You Experiencing Wilderness Thinking?

When we drift away from a close relationship with God we wind up going through the motions. We continue for some time to act like Christians, in that we attend church and stay involved in helping and serving but it doesn't satisfy the deepest longings of our heart. Wanderers often feel forsaken by God. Because we have been blind to His activity or deaf to His voice for some time, we feel abandoned. We think God doesn't care. Do you ever ask yourself these questions?

- I feel like I'm doing all the right things—I teach, I sing, I give, I bring a pie to everything—why don't I ever sense His presence?

- Was my conversion real? Or was I riding an emotional wave?

- If God is in control of my life, why do bad things happen to me?

- Where is this joy the preacher keeps talking about?

- Other than an abundance of disappointments, what's so "abundant" about my life?

Many believers ask themselves these questions. For the Christian who is experiencing spiritual drift, this type of thinking begins to take a foothold, opening the door to doubt that can shove its way in and start to take over. Mature believers deal with these same questions too. But the reason they are able to forge ahead in their faith and not go spinning off into the wilderness is because they know where to go when doubts arise. They go to the heavenly Father in prayer. Instead of hiding from Him like the self-protecting, fearful wanderer does, the mature believer approaches God with confidence and simply lays these doubts at His feet.

Are You Experiencing Wilderness Feelings?

- God seems silent. Why doesn't He speak to me? *I feel alone.*

- Where did God go? I used to feel close to Him. *I feel abandoned.*

- How could God let such a terrible thing happen to me? I thought He was supposed to protect me from harm! *I feel betrayed.*

- Why doesn't God protect me from all these troubles? Maybe He's powerless and not in control. *I feel afraid.*

- I've been away from God for so long that even if He is real, I don't think He'll ever want me back. *I feel guilty.*

- Even if I could find my way back to God, I'm sure He could never work through me again. *I feel unworthy.*

If you are experiencing any of these feelings, ask yourself if this is where you want to stay. How long have you felt this way?

Have you almost given up hope? Do you feel guilty for what you perceive as "lost years" of faith? I did. It took me a long time to understand that my years in the spiritual wilderness had a purpose. They were not meant to be wasted. God planned to use my wilderness experience to bring hope to other wanderers. But before I could become part of His redemptive plan, He needed to get me out! In order to do that He had to wake me up to the reality of how far I had drifted off course.

CHAPTER THREE

The Wake-Up Call

The voice of the Lord shakes the wilderness.
King David

Every wise workman takes his tools away from the work from time to time that they may be ground and sharpened; so does the only-wise Jehovah take his ministers oftentimes away into darkness and loneliness and trouble, that he may sharpen and prepare them for harder work in his service.
Robert Murray M'Cheyne

*W*inter blew in early that year, and the weather mirrored the state of my soul—bleak. I had been Christmas shopping and was already feeling blue. It was hard to focus on the Reason for the season in the midst of chaotic malls, jingling Santas, and the millions of details that crowd out truly embracing the spirit of the Child born in a stable. The further I drifted in my spiritual relationship, the harder it was to celebrate the birth of Christ.

As I pulled into the driveway that dreary December afternoon, nature revealed something that had been hidden by several snowfalls. A warm Chinook wind had uncovered the latest "offerings" from a neighborhood dog—we'll call him "Pal." I dislike confrontation, so I had allowed this distasteful situation to continue for years unchecked. I had kept silent, but my resentment had steadily built. I stomped into the house—grabbed rubber gloves, a grocery bag, and a garden trowel. With mounting frustration, I scraped and scooped. When I finished the bag was heavy. Instead of tossing it in the trash, something snapped in my fevered brain and I acted on a rash impulse.

Back inside the house, I penned a note:

> Dear Bill,*
>
> Inside this bag is something that may belong to you. I am sure it is not mine since I don't own a dog. I know you let Pal roam the streets after midnight and I am tired of cleaning up his mess.
> No hard feelings intended.
> Your neighbor,
> Connie
> PS—If this is not yours then please forgive me.

I attached the note to the bag, left the bag on Bill's doorstep, and scuttled home. I waited for a sign that Bill had gotten the message. I half expected an apologetic phone call. Or maybe a repentant note dropped onto my doorstep. But days passed, and all that happened was Bill no longer waved, smiled, or called out a greeting if we happened to see each other in the neighborhood. He snubbed me.

One of my sisters called shortly after the Doggie Drop, and I told her the whole story, ending with, "So I left the goodie bag on his doorstep with a signed note attached."

---

* Not his real name.

"You didn't!" she blurted.

"I did," I replied. "Why should I have to clean up after his dog? Bill is being irresponsible! If he wants to let his dog roam free he should live in the country. I think he owes me an apology, but instead he's giving me the cold shoulder. Why should I feel guilty?"

Do you feel guilty? a Voice whispered in my ear.

No way! I declared to the heavens.

The next day I hurried out to meet my walking partner, Linda. Although she says she respects my beliefs, she doesn't share them. I launched into the whole dog saga again, unknowingly still seeking absolution. "It's Bill's dog, not mine. People shouldn't have dogs if they don't want to clean up after them! So why should I feel guilty?" were my last words.

Do you feel guilty? I heard again in my mind.

Not one bit! I proclaimed silently.

~~~

Christmas Eve arrived. The family we invited to join us for our traditional French Canadian meal was new in their faith. Jim was a police officer. After dishing up, I took advantage of my audience and asked, "Isn't there some kind of law against letting a dog mess in other people's yards?"

Jim looked up from scooping cranberries onto his meat pie and raised an eyebrow questioningly.

"I think people should be held responsible to clean up after their pets!" I declared roundly.

After wiping his mustache with a napkin, Jim rephrased my original query. "So you want to know if one of your neighbors is breaking some kind of law by letting his dog mess in your yard?"

I nodded, mouth too full of pastry to reply. Already I could sense I wasn't going to like Jim's answer.

"No," he replied. "There isn't a law like that. But if you are having this problem with a neighbor, the best thing to do is talk to him about it."

Not wanting to hear such common sense, I told my story for a third time, in more colorful detail so even an idiot could figure out who was the good guy and who was the bad guy. "He had it coming! Why should I feel guilty?" was my resounding and familiar last word.

Do you feel guilty? was the now familiar rejoinder in my head.

For the third and final time, I denied it: *I do not!* At that moment, I may have heard a cock crow!

Weeks passed. My relationship with Bill remained as cool as the season. I continued to think he should apologize first. One day in February I conducted a telephone interview for a magazine article with a man we'll call Hank, who lives in another province. I was writing a feature story about the children's ministry he had instituted. I asked Hank to mail me his picture for the magazine. He agreed and asked for my address.

When I named my town, he gasped. "You don't have a (well-known franchise) there do you?"

I knew that Bill owned that business and had formerly lived in the same town as Hank. "We do," I admitted, feeling uneasy.

"You don't happen to know a guy named Bill, do you?"

"As a matter of fact, Bill is my neighbor."

"Well, I'll be! I've been praying for him for years. He used to run the (same) business here. I worried when he moved away and we lost touch, but I can see that God had everything under control. Bill moved in next door to a Christian!"

"Yeah," I responded with a brittle laugh. "Isn't God amazing?"

Secretly I was relieved that Hank and Bill had lost touch

because I shuddered to think what Bill would say to his old friend about his neighbor who had left an early "Christmas gift" on his doorstep. I hung up the phone and put my head in my hands. Although I was still too far adrift to feel much shame, I did get the message: Not only was I not making a positive impact for Christ, I was damaging His reputation. For the first time I saw how far I had drifted, and I was shocked.

A Story of Spiritual Blindness

In chapter 9 of John's Gospel, Jesus and His disciples pass a beggar. The man, who is blind, does not know the Son of God is so near. He does not call out to Jesus as He goes by. Rather, Jesus notices him first: "As Jesus was walking along, he saw a man who had been born blind" (John 9:1 NCV). There are times in our spiritual pilgrimage when we call out to God from a heart of desperation. There are also times when, because of our spiritual blindness, we do not even know He is near. But He sees us. And instead of passing us by, He stops and reaches out to us.

The disciples saw the blind man too, and they asked the Rabbi whose sin was responsible for this man's affliction. Jesus replied, "It is not this man's sin or his parents' sin that made him be blind. This man was born blind so that God's power could be shown in him" (9:3 NCV). Does this answer jar you the way it did me when I was a wanderer? In other words, *This man endured the difficulty and shame of blindness—was reduced to begging because he couldn't work—just so Jesus could come along and heal him in a "teachable moment"? That's cruel!* The skeptical mind of a wanderer interprets this as typical of a capricious Deity. *God doesn't really care about us. We're just pawns in His cosmic game. Some He blinds, others He cripples. There's no rhyme or reason. No justice.*

Now, with spiritual sight restored, I see His answer in a different light. We are all like this blind man in that we all have afflictions of some kind that slow our progress, hinder our success, trip us up. Some of those afflictions are physical—crippling arthritis, diabetes, scoliosis, cerebral palsy. Some are addictions—substance abuse, nicotine, caffeine, food. Some are emotional, mental, or psychological—depression, phobias, low intelligence. Some are familial or relational—handicapped children, aging parents, poor social skills, divorce. Some are economic—low income, financial ruin, accumulated debt. Some are spiritual—unbelief, fear, loss of trust. Satan uses our handicaps against us to try to silence our witness. But if we allow Jesus to have His way with us, like this man born blind, we have the potential of being a bold witness. When that happens, "God's power" is shown in us.

Who's Got the Vision Problem?

After the healing, the blind man's neighbors were astonished; some weren't sure it was the same man who had grown up next door to them, even though he kept insisting, "I'm the one!" (9:9). The religious professionals (Pharisees) refused to believe in the face of irrefutable evidence—the man's parents testified that their son had been blind from birth and could now see. God is at work right there in front of them, in their very midst, but nobody sees it; nobody but the blind man. This scripture holds great hope for recovering wanderers. Once Jesus touches our blind eyes and restores our spiritual sight, we see Him for who He really is. And we cannot help but tell others.

The Pharisees questioned the formerly blind man: "How did you get your sight?" His answer is beautiful in its simplicity: "He put mud on my eyes, I washed, and now I see" (9:15 NCV). An argument then broke out among members of the religious elite because this event took place on the Sabbath. Work of any kind—even healing!—was verboten. Some claimed that if Jesus were from God He wouldn't have broken God's laws (that is, worked on the Sabbath). Others argued that healing was a good thing—duh!—and that Jesus must have gotten His power from God because Satan doesn't empower people for good. They could not agree, so they asked the healed man a second time, "'What do you say about him since it was your eyes he opened?' The man answered, 'He is a prophet'" (verse 17 NCV).

The Jews still refused to believe the man had been blind so they called in his parents and questioned them. Afraid of being shunned in their faith community, they answer tentatively: "We know that this is our son and that he was born blind. But we don't know how he can now see. We don't know who opened his eyes. Ask him. He is old enough to speak for himself" (verses 20-21 NCV). So once again the Jews question the formerly blind man, warning him "to give God the glory by telling the truth. We know that this man [Jesus] is a sinner" (verse 24 NCV).

I love the beggar's reply. His frustration over the Pharisees' penchant for making such a simple thing so complex resounds in his words: "I don't know if he is a sinner. One thing I do know: I was blind, and now I see" (verse 25 NCV). Wanderer, think back to your conversion. Remember when God gave you spiritual sight for the first time. In your wilderness experience, you have fallen prey to Satan's lies that "it never happened. It wasn't real." Like this healed blind man, even though you have gone through (or are in) a season of not knowing the true identity of your Savior, you do know one thing. You were once blind and He gave you sight. It's as simple as that.

Just Tell the Truth

The Pharisees, still not satisfied, continue the questioning until finally the healed man has had enough. Completely fed up with their obstinate refusal to believe the truth, he puts on the mantle of his new calling and begins to preach.

> This is a very strange thing. You don't know where he comes from, and yet he opened my eyes. We all know that God does not listen to sinners, but he listens to anyone who worships and obeys him. [Oooh—good one!] Nobody has ever heard of anyone giving sight to a man born blind. [Here's the clincher.] If this man were not from God, he could do nothing (verses 30-33 NCV).

What a transformation! This guy, who did not even call out as Jesus passed by, is now preaching to the religious elite. And what is his message? He tells the plain and simple truth of what this man named Jesus had done for him. Wanderer, that is your calling. That is the hope for your future bold witness.

After the formerly blind man "tells it like he sees it" (pun intended), he gets turfed from the synagogue. Jesus, hearing about it, seeks him out a second time. This time He makes sure there is no doubt about His identity: "The Son of Man is the one talking with you." The healed man replied, "Lord, I believe!" and "worshiped Jesus" (verses 37-38 NCV). This is another valuable point. The blind man, touched by the healing hand of Jesus, boldly witnesses even before he fully understands who the Healer is. While still thinking Jesus was no more than a prophet, he bravely speaks truth in the face of ridicule and pressure to keep silent.

This is also the way it works for the wanderer. As you will see as you read further, God seeks out the blinded wanderer—more than once—and calls him back into relationship. Long before the wanderer fully recognizes Him in all His glory, he obeys. He goes.

He speaks the truth. And in the process, Jesus makes Himself so real, so obvious, that the wanderer is finally able to believe and to worship. What hope!

Some Pharisees were close at hand and overheard Jesus' interchange with the healed man. They asked, "Are you saying we are blind, too?" "If you were blind," Jesus replied, "you would not be guilty of sin. But since you keep saying you see, your guilt remains" (verses 40-41 NCV). There are two key elements here. The first is this: The reason the blind man can see is that he admitted he was blind. When God issues a wake-up call, all He is looking for is an honest answer. Are you blind? If you admit it, there's hope. The second point is, Christians who adamantly take pride in their "seeing status" rather than admitting their blindness and their guilt are hypocrites. The reason I felt guilty every time I told the story of my response to my neighbor's dog is because I *was* guilty. Claiming to be a Christian, claiming to "see" God, I was in fact oblivious to His work all around me.

The humiliating incident between my neighbor and me illustrates how God alerted me to the reality of my spiritual drift. The problem was not that God had abandoned me or that He had quit working—rather, I had drifted so far from Him that, when He worked right before my eyes, I did not even notice. I went around claiming to "see," but I was no more than a Pharisee; my spiritual life had been reduced to rituals. I was a hypocrite.

Responding to the Wake-Up Call

There is no better example in Scripture of a wake-up call than what occurred between King David and the prophet Nathan. Nathan told the king a story:

There were two men in a certain city, one rich and the

other poor. The rich man had a large number of sheep and cattle, but the poor man had nothing except one small ewe lamb that he had bought. It lived and grew up with him and his children. It shared his meager food and drank from his cup; it slept in his arms, and it was like a daughter to him. Now a traveler came to the rich man, but the rich man could not bring himself to take one of his own sheep or cattle to prepare for the traveler who had come to him. Instead, he took the poor man's lamb and prepared it for his guest (2 Samuel 12:1-5).

David was enraged. He declared, "As surely as the Lord lives, the man who did this deserves to die! Because he has done this thing and shown no pity, he must pay four lambs for that lamb" (verse 6).

Then came the clincher: "You are the man!" said the prophet (verse 7).

In case you don't know the background to this accusation, Nathan fills in the gap for us as he makes sure David clearly understands the gravity of his sin:

This is what the Lord God of Israel says: "I anointed you king over Israel, and I delivered you from the hand of Saul. I gave your master's house to you and your master's wives into your arms, and I gave you the house of Israel and Judah, and if that was not enough, I would have given you even more. Why then have you despised the command of the Lord by doing what I consider evil? You struck down Uriah the Hittite with the sword and took his wife [Bathsheba] as your own wife—you murdered him with the Ammonite's sword. Now therefore, the sword will never leave your house because you despised Me and took the wife of Uriah the Hittite to be your own wife" (verses 8-10).

David does not deny his sin. He does not make excuses. He doesn't argue his case or try to tell his side of the story. He agrees he has sinned, and he takes full responsibility. Waking up to the truth, he responds, "I have sinned against the Lord" (verse 13). Pouring out his sorrow, he cries out to God:

> Be gracious to me, God,
> according to Your faithful love;
> According to Your abundant compassion,
> blot out my rebellion.
> Wash away my guilt,
> and cleanse me from my sin.
> For I am conscious of my rebellion,
> and my sin is always before me.
> Against You—You alone—I have sinned
> and done this evil in Your sight.
> So You are right when You pass sentence;
> You are blameless when You judge (Psalm 51:1-4).

The difference between heeding and overlooking a wake-up call can be seen in the wanderer's response to it. If we shrug off the spiritual tap on the shoulder and keep drifting, what could have been a wake-up call and a turning point becomes nothing more than another bump in the road. However, if we stop our headlong pursuit and admit, "I'm lost…and I don't know the way back," there's hope. As soon as we admit the truth of our situation and call for help to the unseen God, the first "course correction" has occurred.

> The wake-up call is not the solution
> to the problem—it is simply the gateway
> to the path leading to healing and restoration.
> It is a chance for the wanderer to turn Godward.

If you are experiencing a season of wilderness, God may have already sent you some wake-up calls, but you've missed them. How can you recognize such a call? Anytime you see yourself for who you really are and admit you have drifted off course, this is a wake-up call. This next point is vital: The wake-up call is not the solution to the problem—it is simply the gateway to the path leading to healing and restoration. It is a chance for the wanderer to turn Godward. The wake-up call does not change you; you respond to it, and *God* changes you.

෬෬෬

The cobblestone path that leads from the wilderness of dry faith into the garden of His presence is constructed, stone by stone, with Godward choices. Each of these stones is a small *yes*. Each *yes* puts another stone on the path in front of you. You say *yes* to what appears to be God even though you are still quite shaky in being able to recognize His involvement in your life. This is a period of true faith. Every *yes* is an act of faith. But it's slow going. It's baby steps. If you try to run ahead, you'll run out of cobblestones and get bogged down in drifting sand again.

The wake-up call, once heeded, can become a literal turning point. It can be the point at which the wanderer turns toward God, seeking forgiveness and restoration. Don't be misled; there is no quick fix. Restoration can take weeks, months, or years. We don't wander into the wilderness of dry faith overnight. Similarly, we don't recover instantaneously. Patterns of thought and feeling must change; habits need breaking and reforming. But the journey of recovery is a better place than the wilderness. Glimpses of the living God become the oases in the desert that sustain the thristy wanderer and keep him traveling Godward.

If you sense God is trying to wake you up, pay attention. Agree with Him that you have sinned and have wandered away from His presence. Admit that you are blind but have been claiming to see for a long time. Ask Him to restore your sight. And then, like that blind man who stumbled along with mud on his eyes, heading for the pool of Siloam, begin to walk by faith again. Your full sight will not be restored for some time, but don't lose hope. He will heal you.

CHAPTER FOUR

Thou Shalt Have No Other Gods

Forget the former things; do not dwell on the past. See I am
doing a new thing! Now it springs up; do you not perceive it?
I am making a way in the desert and streams in the wasteland.
God speaking through the prophet Isaiah

Perhaps we should encourage pastors and others to publicly
admit when they don't feel God's presence and to describe the
agony and confusion and sense of deep letdown that
strangles their souls during those dark nights. It is
a normal experience. It is part of a good journey.
Larry Crabb

*L*ynne grew up in church. Her desire to help people led her to college, seeking a degree in social work. However, she grew disillusioned with the idea of helping people with their physical needs while ignoring their spiritual needs. After college, she veered away from social work. But she was also disillusioned with the church of her childhood, for although it did much to address the spiritual needs of people, it did little to address their physical needs.

Though she had read the Bible since childhood, she turned to it again at the age of 21, "as if reading it for the first time." She was completely captivated by what she read in the Gospels and the Acts of the Apostles. She became enamored with the vision of what the church could be. Not long after that she visited a friend who had an exciting youth ministry in Chicago. This young man had a vision for the church and a zeal for the Lord that matched her own. They fell in love, and she married Bill Hybels; a year later they started Willow Creek Community Church in a suburb of Chicago.[1]

Together, they threw themselves into the work, devoting their lives to the growth of the kingdom. Lynne tried very hard—and succeeded—at being a "good" pastor's wife. She took care to be the model Christian she thought a pastor's wife should be. Rebellion was the furthest thing from her mind because she sincerely wanted to honor God and her calling. Every day she would cry out to God, "Tell me what you want me to do today, and I'll do it. Anything!" Frustrated, she never seemed to hear a clear answer to that plea. She redoubled her efforts, working harder than ever in an attempt to earn God's favor. Over time, she began to suffer the effects of physical, emotional, and spiritual exhaustion.

She slid into depression. After 15 years as a pastor's wife, Lynne awoke to the reality that something terrible had happened, and she didn't know how to fix it. She still loved the church, but she hated her life. Desperate, she walked into the office of a Christian counselor and asked for help. "Every night when I go to bed I pray I won't wake up in the morning," she told the counselor. "But I have two kids who I adore and I don't want to leave them motherless."

She was 39 years old...and she "felt like a complete failure."

With the help of counseling and the full support of her husband, over the next ten years, she embarked on a journey of self-discovery, spiritual renewal, and healing. Eventually, she found freedom in Christ. Piece by piece she had to dismantle her unhealthy, unbalanced life and build a new life based on the truth of who God really is—not who she always thought He was.

The reason I include Lynne Hybels's story is because people like you and me—everyday Christians—are tempted to dismiss "big name" believers as people we can't relate to. We put the Lynne and Bill Hybelses of the world on pedestals, assuming God must give them an extra measure of grace in accordance with the impact of their public endeavors. Not so. Lynne Hybels is no different from you or me. She has no hotline to heaven; she uses the same access we do—prayer.

However, there is one difference. We tend to look up to those who are in the public eye and expect them to model the stellar life of faith for us. To show us how it's done. I'm as guilty of this "celebrity awe" as many of you are. With that in mind, when I heard Lynne's honest vulnerability as she courageously told her wilderness story, I had two thoughts. One: *If someone "famous" like Lynne can slip into spiritual drift, then maybe I'm not so weird.* Suddenly I didn't feel like such a schmuck! Two: *If someone as well-known as Lynne can shatter the conspiracy of silence and tell the truth, then I have no excuse for keeping silent.* Nor do you. Lynne's honesty encourages me to live authentically.

Recognizing the False God

Lynne Hybels admits that the view of God she had developed when growing up was faulty. "I had a toxic relationship with God," she says. She was a sensitive child who grew up hearing messages of hellfire and brimstone. That teaching formed in her impressionable mind an erroneous picture of who God was. She thought of Him as a hard-hearted taskmaster. She believed she would have to work very hard and be very good in order to please Him. So that's what she tried to do, because she truly wanted to please God. Eventually, her determination to *earn* God's love in order to *feel* His love left her completely exhausted. What she needed most of all was rest—but "*my* God wouldn't let me rest," she says.

In 1991, Lynne realized the only way she was going to get the rest she needed in order to survive was to "get rid of *my* God," as she puts it. Staring up into the endless blue of a hot summer sky as she stretched out on the deck of a little sailboat, she told God she was done with Him—"I can't do it anymore. I can't keep striving for your love." At that time, God felt like a horrible weight, and she knew she could "no longer carry the burden of a harsh and demanding deity."

Her world didn't stop turning and let her off. Her life was still full of responsibilities. But instead of continuing to work and strive and push herself, whenever possible, she collapsed into a recliner and stared out her family-room window at the changing seasons. "Although I felt guilty, I had no energy for anything else," she notes.

The Gospel of Grace

The apostle Paul's pre–Damascus road understanding of God sounds similar to Lynne's. Prior to his conversion, Saul zealously worked to fulfill all the laws of his Jewish tradition, and then some. He took it upon himself to pursue Christ's followers to their deaths. However, once he encountered the risen Lord en route to Damascus, Saul, now Paul, was forever changed. "I have been crucified with Christ and I no longer live but Christ lives in me," he testifies. "I have died to the law, that I might live to God" (Galatians 2:19-20).

After some years as a missionary, Paul became frustrated with Jewish Christians who clung to old traditions, like circumcision, and included then as necessary parts of salvation. In Galatians 2 he tells how he opposed Cephas (Peter) in front of the believers at Antioch. Apparently Peter "used to eat with the Gentiles before certain men came from James. However, when they came, he withdrew and separated himself, because he feared those from the circumcision party" (verse 12). Peter's actions had dire consequences, according to Paul, because then "the rest of the Jews joined his hypocrisy, so that even Barnabas was carried away by their hypocrisy (verse 13). In the most telling of his arguments, he proclaims, "I do not set aside the grace of God; for if righteousness comes through the law, then Christ died for nothing" (verse 21). This passage fairly screams, *Do you get it? We are saved by grace, not by the law. That's why Jesus came!* He repeats the same message further on in his letter: "For as many of you as have been baptized into Christ have put on Christ. There is no Jew or Greek, slave or free, for you are all one in Christ Jesus" (3:27-28).

Why do we preach and believe the gospel of grace but live by the law? Paul was upset because, while he agreed that Jews should preserve their tradition and culture, when the "circumcision party" followed rules that clearly flouted Jesus' teaching of total equality under God, they were missing the point. In frustration he declares,

> Christ has liberated us into freedom. Therefore stand firm and don't submit again to a yoke of slavery. Take note! I, Paul, tell you that if you get circumcised, Christ will not benefit you at all. Again I testify to every man who gets circumcised that he is obligated to keep the entire law. You who are trying to be justified by the law

are alienated from Christ; you have fallen from grace! (Galatians 5:1-4).

When they expected Gentiles to follow Jewish tradition as part of the "salvation package," they were adding things to the gospel that Jesus did not teach. Also, the circumcision party was distracting people from the gospel message of grace and confusing them with their hypocrisy.

Finding the Biblical God

If believers in Bible times struggled in their perception of who God was and what He wanted them to do, then we should not be surprised when we, 20 centuries later, face the same hurdle. What we all need to recognize is that some of the perceptions we have about God come from church tradition, from culture, from our parents, from secular and religious media, from books, from the people we associate with, from experiences we've had—and so on, ad infinitum.

Lynne Hybels came to a point in her faith journey where in desperation she decided that, to survive, she had to walk away from God as she understood Him. Thankfully, the God she walked away from wasn't the God she later came to know and love. Rather, she left behind her toxic view of a harsh and demanding deity that was crushing her under the weight of its demands. Resting in her recliner by the window, she "watched squirrels chase each other as the leaves turned to gold, and an amazing thing happened."

As she yielded to the beauty of God's creation, she began to long for "a God" again. But not the God of her childhood.

"It's me," she whispered into the void as she opened her heart's door just a crack.

"I love you," she heard, in a whisper as soft as her own. "I want you to rest, to listen, to watch. All those years you worked so hard, I was trying to get you to slow down."

Lynne describes this experience as the pivotal moment of her life, the place where she was truly embraced by the love of God. Her expression of poignant longing struck a chord within me. As Christians, we so deeply yearn to hear the Father speak words of love to us. We work and serve and knock ourselves out in order to earn His favor, all the while preaching the gospel of grace (unearned merit). But in our deepest place, in the hidden parts of our soul, we hunger for His tender voice. We thirst for His whispers of love. We long for His healing touch. Lynne says she still weeps every time she tells or writes this part of her story.

Lynne reports that her depression and exhaustion were the best things that ever happened to her. Now she begins every day silent, waiting before God. "I empty my mind of words and thoughts and invite God to enter. I fall into the well of His love," she says. Now, her efforts flow from fullness, from joy and from gratitude for life. "My life is grounded in a true daily experience of Him."

Lynne's story is compelling because she went the extra mile. She didn't quit. I know many people—and so do you—who say they "used to be Christians." People who, for a vast array of reasons, decided to walk away from God and the church. But Lynne, even though she was at the end of her endurance, left a door of possibility slightly ajar, and the warm glow of the Father's presence peeped through that crack and connected with her. Lynne stayed open to the chance that maybe "her God" was a false god...and that the true God really existed and was waiting to be discovered.

The Positive Side of Doubt

Carol Kent, in *Tame Your Fears,* echoes the thoughts Lynne and I have:

> Doubts about God need not lead to denial, defeat, bitterness, or escape. Instead they can lead to a "truth search." Asking questions related to our doubts will lead to a strengthened faith as we discover truth in the process.[2]

My husband told me the same thing many times during my years in the wilderness. Every time I spoke of my frustration and the fear I had lost my faith, his reply was, "Connie, you haven't lost your faith, you're simply finding *your own* faith." Like Lynne, I was in the process of shedding a toxic view of God and in search of the true God of Scripture. Like Lynne, it did not happen overnight but took many years. I suspect that many of the "former believers" we know were laboring under a false notion of who God is. In frustration and confusion, too many of them walked away from a relationship with Him before going the extra mile.

Letting God Be Who He Is

I have a 40-something friend named Laurie, a young Christian. She is divorced, having survived more than one physically abusive partner. She began making poor choices in her early teens, abusing her mind, body, and spirit with alcohol and drugs. She suffered emotional abuse early on from an unloving mother and a critical father. She was gang-raped as a teenager. She almost froze to death when she collapsed, drunk, on a stranger's doorstep one winter night years ago.

Thankfully, she's a survivor. Her personal tragedies drew her toward a forgiving, loving God. Like the returning prodigal, one day she came to her senses and crawled into the arms of a gracious Father. However, some habits that she picked up along the way still plague her.

Laurie is a smoker. She quits every few weeks but always starts up again. She seldom drinks anymore, but when she does, she occasionally overdoes it. Although she is seeking a long-term relationship based on mutual love, commitment, and respect, she winds up in short-term relationships based on physical attraction and mutual need.

Maybe because she knows I love her and am also utterly dependent on Grace, she talks to me about her life. Perhaps she wants a safe "confessional." I'm not sure. Each time she tells me her story, she invites me into her life, and I am grateful to be asked.

We all have Lauries in our life. What do we say to them? What does Jesus say? What did He say to the woman caught in adultery? The spiritual police caught this woman in the act and, wanting to trap Jesus, dragged her in front of Him as He was teaching in the Temple courts.

> They forced her to stand before the people. They said to Jesus, "Teacher, this woman was caught having sexual relations with a man who is not her husband. The law of Moses commands that we stone to death every woman who does this. What do you say we should do?" (John 8:3-5 NCV).

If this isn't a setup, I don't know what is. Think about it. How did they chance upon someone, in the middle of the day, in this compromising situation? Did they go door to door, hoping to stumble upon the jackpot? Sheesh! The whole thing smells of trickery and deceit. We'll never know, because Scripture doesn't explain how the spiritual police were "lucky enough" to find this pitiful pawn for their evil scheme—only that they did and dragged her into public in her shameful state. And there they stood encircling her, like vultures ready to feed off the carcass.

Instead of answering their trick question, Jesus bent over and wrote in the sand. The Scripture does not tell us what He wrote, but many scholars have taken their best shot at making educated guesses. I'm inclined to agree with those who think He listed a few sins being practiced by the mob who already had stones in hand, ready to do their religious duty. When He finally spoke, He said, "Anyone here who has never sinned can throw the first stone at her" (verse 7 NCV). Then He bent over and wrote some more.

Guess what happened? People started drifting away. I think it is so significant that the Gospel states the first ones to leave were the *older men*. There's something to be said for wisdom coming with age. Soon, the gang had all dissipated like sand seeping through a crack. Left alone with the woman, Jesus straightened up and asked her where all her accusers were. She reported the obvious; they're all gone. "Neither do I condemn you," Jesus said to her. "Go, and from now on do not sin any more" (verse 11).

Like the "older men" in the crowd, I am one who has lived long enough to recognize the truth about my sinful heart. I have habits that plague and haunt and grip my life. Because my weaknesses are different from those of the adulterous woman, does that make me any better? Not in God's eyes.

Like the crowd that gathered, ready to stone the woman caught in adultery, I come face-to-face with Truth every time my friend Laurie confesses a personal failing. I hang my head in shame at my own sin, and I walk away from condemnation. And Laurie is left alone with Him—with the only One who has the power to help her change. Sometimes Christians just need to get out of the way and let Jesus be the God we profess to believe He is!

∾ ∾ ∾

Who is God, really? In the process of trying to figure that out, I'm learning who He isn't. He is not the harsh and demanding deity Lynne and I once thought He was. Rather than being condemning, He is welcoming. He is restoring. He comes looking for us in our spiritual blindness and gives us sight. God's nature is too vast for me to understand, but the God I am beginning to know is a God who pursues. He is personal. He is trustworthy. He is full of grace. His love is boundless and endless. He asks for my obedience because He knows what's best for me. He asks for my surrender because He knows that is where I will find true freedom. Travel a little further with me as I tell stories—some you know, some you don't—that will shed light on this quest to discover the real God.

Part Two

Sonrise:
Discover the Real God

CHAPTER FIVE

The God Who Pursues

You did not abandon them in the wilderness
because of Your great compassion.
The prayer of Nehemiah

I sought the Lord, and afterward I knew
He moved my soul to seek Him, seeking me;
It was not I that found, O Savior true,
No, I was found of Thee.
Anonymous

$\mathcal{H}$ermann Brandt was born and raised in South Africa. With his movie-star Afrikaner good looks and winsome personality, he never lacked for companionship. He was raised in church and considered himself to be a Christian from a young age. As a teen he began to pull away, to go his own way. The church's rules and regulations squeezed his artistic free spirit, and he wanted space to explore other options.

Hermann went off to college and leapt into the bohemian lifestyle, embracing it with fervor. He met a statuesque blonde named Wilmien, and they fell in love. When talk of marriage began, Hermann told Wilmien about his family's values and that he did not want to marry an unbeliever. She did not know what he meant by a personal relationship with Christ, so Hermann took her home to meet his family, and there his brother-in-law Sias explained the gospel to her.

Wilmien welcomed Jesus into her life, accepted the good news with all her heart, and was immediately changed. Without realizing what her newfound, vibrant faith would mean on a day-to-day basis, Hermann happily announced their engagement, and they were soon married. That's when the trouble started.

He discovered that his new bride wasn't as much fun as she had been before. She wanted to go to church, grow in her faith, and socialize with other believers—and he wanted none of that. They drifted further and further apart and were at the point of breakup when, out of the blue, Wilmien got pregnant. She knew how shaky her marriage was and had not planned on bringing a child into such uncertainty, but here was this gorgeous blond baby boy with startling blue eyes and a heart-wrenching smile, and suddenly Hermann couldn't leave. He fell deeply in love with his son, and even though his wife made him furious with her "religious fanaticism," he didn't have the heart to walk away from his little boy.

༄ ༄ ༄

Ten years into the marriage, Hermann, Wilmien, and little Carl found themselves in the USA on a work visa, where Wilmien was under contract as an occupational therapist. Hermann had seen more than one creative business venture fail, and he spent most of his time caring for Carl and pursuing his hedonistic passions in his spare time. The marriage was miserable, as Wilmien and Hermann did not see eye-to-eye on anything, including whether or not she should take Carl to church. Hermann said, "No way!" remembering what a burden it had been to him as a child. Wilmien wept but acquiesced.

Amazingly, throughout that decade of disappointment and betrayal and suffering, she knew one thing. God had called her to be submissive. So even though Hermann's demands were sometimes against everything she believed, she always tried to obey and have a gentle spirit. But over time, she was being worn down and was starting to feel desperate. Driving home from work, she would cry out to God to make Himself known to her husband and change her circumstances. And God would say to her, *What about you?* She could never judge, because God always called her to look first to her own life and to submit to Him and to her husband.

One night Hermann arrived home late, wild-eyed and open-mouthed.

"What happened to you?" Wilmien asked, feeling a surge of terror. She lived in constant fear that Hermann would abandon her and Carl in this foreign land, where she was bound by her contract and could not leave.

"I don't know," Hermann muttered. He brushed past her and went to the bedroom. He stayed there for five days, rising only to take Carl to school in the morning and pick him up again at the end of the day.

Wilmien grew more and more afraid, until on the fifth day she was near panic. Late that night, her husband came to her and asked her to sit beside him on the bed because he wanted to talk. She dreaded what was coming but prayed for strength and steeled her nerves.

"Wilmien," he began, slowly and quietly, "five days ago, the Lord came to me. He has asked me to be righteous. And to commit myself to you. And that is what I am doing right now."

Wilmien was facing the mirror on the bureau as she perched on the edge of the bed opposite Hermann. She saw tears shoot straight out of her eyes as he said the words she had longed to hear for a decade. They held each other for a long time. After the storm of weeping had passed, he told her his story.

∾∾∾

Wilmien already knew that as a college student, Hermann had gotten fed up with God as he knew Him because the lure of the world was too strong to resist. Hermann had had what he thought was his last conversation with God at that time—he'd said, "I'm tired of trying to live for You. It doesn't satisfy. If You want me, You'll have to come after me because I'm finished with You." He was pretty sure God would never take him up on his challenge, and he headed off into the tangle of worldly pursuits. Wilmien knew firsthand the suffering that her husband's choices had wrought in their marriage and in her heart.

Hermann then recounted his experience of five days earlier. While listening to a business presentation in a nearby city, he thought he heard an inner voice calling him: *Hermann, I love you just like you love Carl. This much I love you, but so much more!* The voice continued: *Everything you are looking for—joy, peace, fulfillment—you'll find in Me. But I want one thing. You must be righteous.*

Hermann instantly responded, "Lord, if that's what You're giving, that's what I want!" At that moment, it was as though the heavy stone doors of a dungeon were flung open, flooding the interior with light. "In my mind's eye, I saw a face, smiling at me," he reported.

He sat silent and stunned through the remainder of the conference. After the evening session, he drove home. He felt as if

Jesus were sitting beside him in the car, bringing up his sins one by one. As each sin was revealed, Hermann said, "I confess it." And Jesus tossed it out the window. For three hours, he confessed and was forgiven.

When he arrived home, although he felt completely drained, he knew he was a new man. But he was too afraid to tell anyone what had happened because it was so weird and unbelievable. So he went to bed and stayed there for five days, afraid to speak, wondering if he would ever recover. During those days Hermann was hiding in his room in fear, Satan tormented him day and night, trying to convince him he had only imagined the heavenly visitation. That it never happened. That God was a lie. He cried out in anguish over and over, "Lord, give me peace!"

On the fifth day, he suddenly felt compelled to read Scripture. He did not own a Bible, but he knew just where to find his wife's. He opened it randomly to Luke chapter 19. Verse 42 leapt off the page, and he read it aloud: "If you, even you, had only recognized on this day the things that make for peace! But now they are hidden from your eyes...because you did not recognize the time of your visitation from God."

Jumping to his feet, he shouted, "So it *was* You!" At that moment Satan left him. He continued to read the Bible as God spoke to his spirit. Suddenly Hermann remembered telling God ten years earlier that if He wanted him, He would have to come after him. And so He had.

❧❧❧

Hermann and Wilmien are friends of mine. Their story illustrates how God pursues us, even when we act like we don't want Him to and doubt that He exists. "In the Bible we do not see man groping after God, we see God reaching after man."[1] After Adam and Eve's fall into sin, they tried to hide from God because they were ashamed. But God went looking for them. "Where are you?" He called (Genesis 3:9). And so it is in the world in which we live today. God is still actively in pursuit of His children.

When Hermann issued a challenge to God, he never expected God to take him up on it. Little did he know that God was watching, waiting, and (dare I say?) sometimes weeping as He waited for the right place and the appointed hour when He knew Hermann would hear Him call.

Hermann's story is not new. The psalmist David wrote it centuries ago:

> Where can I go from your Spirit?
> Where can I flee from your presence?
> If I go up to the heavens, you are there;
> if I make my bed in the depths, you are there.
> If I rise on the wings of the dawn,
> if I settle on the far side of the sea,
> even there your hand will guide me,
> your right hand will hold me fast
> (Psalm 139:7-10 NIV).

The fact that we are out of control should not render us hopeless, but rather should remind us that Someone else is in control.

He Comes Looking for Us

For some people the wilderness lasts months—for others, years. "What makes a true dark night a school for the soul is that it goes on and on and on."[2] Some people go through it many times; others are grateful they have had to endure it only once. The common thread that joins recovering wilderness wanderers is they have realized that nothing they can do will "bring God back." The fact that we are out of control should not render us hopeless, but rather should remind us that Someone else is in control. "It is Christ's way to come to us when our coming to Him is out of the question," Spurgeon writes.[3]

In Luke's Gospel the Pharisees and scribes complain that Jesus "welcomes sinners and eats with them" (15:2). In an attempt to make them see His true mission, Jesus tells three stories (parables): those of the lost sheep, the lost coin, and the lost son—the prodigal. All three have the same point: We can run, but we can't hide—God pursues His children.

The Lost Sheep

Jesus' first illustration begins with this question: "What man among you, who has 100 sheep and loses one of them, does not leave the 99 in the open field and go after the lost one until he finds it?" (Luke 15:4). Nowhere in this parable does Jesus say whether or not the lost sheep is already a believer or has yet to be converted. He just says the sheep is lost. If you are, or have been, a wanderer, you feel lost. Like that sheep, you know the Shepherd's voice, but you've wandered out of range. You can't hear it anymore. You think it's your own fault for wandering off, and perhaps it is—so guilt convinces you that the Shepherd will be angry at your carelessness. Not so. Leaving the 99, the shepherd heads out into the wilderness and searches until his effort is rewarded. He finds the wayward sheep.

What happens when the shepherd finds that lost sheep? Does he whack it over the head with His shepherd's crook and call it a "dumb goat" for getting lost? Does he whip it and drive it back to the herd on the double-quick? No!

When he has found it, he joyfully puts it on his shoulders, and coming home, he calls his friends and neighbors together, saying to them, "Rejoice with me, because I have found my lost sheep!" (Luke 15:5-6). He's so happy he throws a party! Then Jesus adds this: "I tell you, in the same way, there will be more joy in heaven over one sinner who repents than over 99 righteous people who don't need repentance" (verse 7).

All heaven rejoices. I still find that hard to grasp. It fills me with humble gratitude and awe that all heaven would care about one lost sheep. But it's true—God deeply cares about the wanderer. He pursues us and doesn't stop until He finds us and carries us back to the fold. Take heart, fellow wanderer. He'll find you. "Your Father in heaven is not willing that any of these little ones should be lost" (Matthew 18:14 NIV).

The Lost Coin

The next story has the same theme. A woman has ten coins. She loses one. She lights a lamp, sweeps the house, and "searches carefully" until she finds it. Like the shepherd, she rejoices when the lost coin is found, calls in the neighbors, and serves coffee and cake. Jesus repeats, "I tell you, in the same way, there is joy in the presence of God's angels over one sinner who repents" (Luke 15:10). Again, not only is there gladness on earth, but heaven rejoices when a sinner turns to God.

The Lost Son

Just in case the Pharisees and scribes missed the point of the first two stories, Jesus takes another run at it with His parable of the prodigal son.

A man had two sons. The younger of them said to his father, "Father, give me the share of the estate I have coming to me." So he distributed the assets to them. Not many days later, the younger son gathered together all he had and traveled to a distant country, where he squandered his estate in foolish living. After he had spent everything, a severe famine struck that country, and he had nothing. Then he went to work for one of the citizens of that country, who sent him into his fields to feed pigs. He longed to eat his fill from the carob pods the pigs were eating, and no one would give him any. But when he came to his senses [heard the wake-up call], he said, "How many of my father's hired hands have more than enough food, and here I am dying of hunger! I'll get up, go to my father, and say to him, 'Father, I have sinned against heaven and in your sight. I'm no longer worthy to be called your son. Make me like one of your hired hands'" (Luke 15:11-19).

This is classic wilderness thinking. *I messed up. I'm bad. I've wandered and squandered, and I don't deserve a relationship with Dad. Hey—wait a minute! I have an idea. Maybe I can work my way back into his good books. Yeah, that's what I'll do. I'll work really hard for a long time, and maybe Dad will notice and he'll beckon me in out of the cold. We can sit around the supper table like we did in the good old days!*

So he got up and went to his father. But while the son was still a long way off, his father saw him and was filled with compassion. He ran, threw his arms around his neck, and kissed him (verse 20).

Read this again—and then tell me who ran. And then tell me how it was that the father saw the son while he was still far off. Obviously he was watching for the son's return. He expected it. He banked on it. The father's first emotion, Jesus says, was compassion. Not anger. Not disgust. Not disappointment.

Those negative feelings aptly describe the wanderer's heart, don't they? Angry at ourselves for squandering precious months or years, we are afraid Dad will punish us. What a shock to find Him watching for our return—and then to feel the strength of His embrace as He catches us before we fall in complete exhaustion from our long journey.

> The son said to him, "Father, I have sinned against heaven and in your sight. I'm no longer worthy to be called your son."
>
> But the father told his slaves, "Quick! Bring out the best robe and put it on him; put a ring on his finger and sandals on his feet. Then bring the fattened calf and slaughter it, and let's celebrate with a feast, because this son of mine was dead and is alive again; he was lost and is found!" So they began to celebrate (verses 21-24).

Can it be any clearer than this? Entire books have been written, masterpieces have been painted, on this beautiful scene where the father welcomes back his wandering son. Not only does he welcome him, it's like he never left. He restores him instantly to full "sonship." Wanderer, we are the prodigals. Why do we doubt His love? God went after Hermann, encountered him in the unlikeliest time and place, and called him back. Similarly, He guided my steps so that, like the sheep that had wandered off, I would come to see and hear Him again. And He is pursuing you too.

God Initiates

Too often we think we have to chase after God, peeking behind curtains, opening doors, squinting through peepholes, searching under beds. *How can I find God?* we worry. But God so desires to connect with us that He comes after us. He finds us wherever we are and calls us to join Him in His work. Whether or not we respond to that call with a *yes*, a willing heart, determines what happens next in our faith journey.[4]

Out of the Blue

A pivotal moment in my wilderness experience began with a shared cup of tea with a friend, a stained-glass artist, who wishes to remain anonymous. Little did I know that the pursuing God was reeling me in. As much as she loves her art, stained glass is not the passion of this woman's life. Jesus is. Her primary enterprise is intercessory prayer. Unbeknownst to me, she prayed regularly for me for some time before telling me about it.

One day in the winter of 2000, she ushered me out of the bitter cold and into her quaint cottage. After a few steaming sips she paused, placed her hands reverently on her Bible, and told me something that would eventually change the course of my life.

"I prostrated myself before the Lord this morning," she began. Her custom was that she never entered her glass studio unless she stayed on her face in worship and prayer until God released her. "And He gave me Psalm 51," she continued. "But He told me this scripture was not for me"—pause, sip, gaze intently—"but it was for you, Connie." She watched to see if I had fully comprehended the immensity of this spiritual transaction.

I nodded and smiled, acting duly impressed even though I was skeptical that anything she had to say could impact my stone-cold heart. After all, I was a wanderer. A pretender. A fake. I wasn't so sure there *was* a God anymore. Then my friend opened her loved-to-tatters Bible and began to read. She took me through all of Psalm 51, stopping here and there to exhort me with certain words or thoughts. The first passage she parked on hit me right where it hurt: "Surely you desire truth in the inner parts" (verse 6 NIV). Boy, did I! I hated my hypocrisy but could not seem to change.

"Create in me a pure heart" (verse 10 NIV), was the next place that grabbed me. Oh, how I longed to be pure! Everything had been so simple in my early days of faith, so black-and-white. But a lot of water had passed under the bridge; my heart and mind were so twisted that I despaired of ever finding peace. She read, "Restore to me the joy of your salvation and grant me a willing spirit to sustain me" (verse 12 NIV). "Isn't this what you want, Connie?" she asked with heartbreaking earnestness. It was exactly what I wanted but was convinced would never again be mine.

Then she asked me to listen carefully because what she was about to say was her message to me from God: "Then I will teach transgressors your ways and sinners will turn back to you" (verse 13 NIV). She stopped, locked onto me with her steely gaze, and said, "This is what you are called to do, Connie dear." She was dead serious. If she hadn't been, I may have burst out laughing. Teach transgressors? *I* was a transgressor! Turn sinners? *I* was a sinner!

In my dark night of the soul I had forgotten that Someone else had been "numbered with the transgressors" (Isaiah 53:5,12 NIV). Though Jesus had not sinned, "God made Him who had no sin to be sin for us, so that in Him we might become the righteousness of God" (2 Corinthians 5:21 NIV). Jesus was a transgressor for my sake as He hung on the cross. However, at that point in my wilderness, I did not identify with Christ, or with any other worthy soul. I just felt terribly empty and guilty.

After more tea and a lengthy time of prayer, I bundled up and was sent on my way with a warm hug. As I trudged homeward, a faint glimmer of hope...an ember of possibility...glowed somewhere deep in my soul. Without knowing I was praying, I mouthed a prayer—it was more like a challenge—to God. *Okay, God. If what she says is true and You are calling me to speak up for You, I will do it. But I won't go looking. If someone calls and asks, then I will say yes.* Unknowingly, I had played right into the hand of a pursuing God!

Prayers Tinged with Blue

Meanwhile, without my knowledge, my friend cut a small piece of blue glass into a triangle shape about four inches high and two inches wide at the bottom. She perched the triangle in her east window. When the sun shone through it in the morning and she spied "the little patch of blue" in her living room, she would pause to pray for me.

Months passed. One day, "out of the blue," I got a call. A friend of a friend had heard I might be a good speaker, so would I fly to Ontario and speak for their women's retreat several months hence? I was stunned by the request, and my first inclination was to refuse. After all, what could I possibly say that would be worth the expense of my travel? Suddenly I remembered my "deal" with God—and with great fear and trepidation said, "Yes." I hung up the phone and wondered if I had lost my mind!

The event organizer sent me details over the ensuing weeks. The first e-mail I received was short and obviously rushed—"I don't have my Bible or my notes in front of me, but I think the scripture is Psalm 56:1. Gotta dash. More later." I turned to that verse: "Be merciful to me, O God, for men hotly pursue me..." Yikes! What was I getting myself into? I grinned at the humor of the obvious misquote. I knew in my heart she had mixed up the numbers and the scripture was actually Psalm 51:6: "Surely you desire truth in the inner parts" (NIV). *Just a coincidence,* I thought.

The phone rang a few weeks later with another invitation. Would I be the keynote speaker for a national women's event to be held in four provinces over four months? Let me explain that I had spoken publicly only rarely up to this point, once per year at most. Suddenly two requests, one after another, arrived—out of the blue. Remembering my promise, I said, "yes." Again I wondered if I should have my head examined!

The event organizer called me and told me the theme: "Restoring Joy." The scripture? "Restore to me the joy of your salvation and grant me a willing spirit to sustain me" (Psalm 51:12 NIV). This was uncanny, but I had heard of lightning striking twice in the same place, so I was still skeptical. (Can you believe it?)

When You Turn Back...

As the time approached for my talks, I grew desperate and called out to God. "We've got a deal here," I railed. "I said *yes*. I did my part. You'd better come through with a message!" Silence. I read Psalm 51 over and over and over. Hearing no clear direction, I sensed that God probably wanted me to tell the truth about my spiritual wilderness. This scared the liver right out of me.

At the first event, I spoke four times. The first three talks, not knowing what else to do, I told funny stories, tossed in a scripture or two, and ran for cover while they clapped. *Just keep them laughing,* I told myself, *and maybe they'll think this mirth is joy and feel like they've found what they came for.* Finally, in the last message, I tagged on the truth about my wilderness journey. I told them I had been there for a long time, I wasn't sure how I'd gotten there or when I would get out. I also told them God was pursuing me. He hadn't abandoned me—He'd connected with me and called me from the midst of the wilderness to speak in His name. I had hope.

The woman who waited for me in the shadows outside my hotel room (see chapter 1), after confessing her own wilderness experience, asked if I had ever considered Luke 22:31. There Jesus says, "Simon, Simon. Satan has asked to sift you as wheat" (NIV). I had not considered it. For the first time, it occurred to me that my decade in the wilderness had a purpose. Could it be that, like Peter, God was allowing me to be sifted so I would have the understanding and the compassion to reach out to other wanderers? Could it be that those dark years would give me and others "a future and a hope"?

Back in my room after that encounter, I opened my Bible to Luke and read further: "I have prayed for you, Simon, that your faith may not fail. And when you have turned back, strengthen your brothers" (22:32 NIV). The similarity of this verse and "teach transgressors your ways and sinners will turn back to you" (Psalm 51:13 NIV) was impossible for me to miss. The latter part of the verse in Luke is what riveted me. Jesus did not say *if*, He said *when* you turn back. Could this mean that, all during my sojourn in the wilderness, Jesus Himself had been praying for me? That He knew I would return?

This lost sheep caught a glimpse of the approaching Shepherd. I felt His touch as He reached out for me to sling me over His shoulders and plod homeward.

CHAPTER SIX

Undying Love

I have loved you with an everlasting love;
therefore, I have continued to extend faithful love to you.
God speaking through the prophet Jeremiah

God has two dwellings: one in heaven,
and the other in a meek and thankful heart.
Izaak Walton

*T*ammy called in the middle of the night. She was hysterical. Her husband had abandoned her and the baby. I went over to her house and made tea. She wept as we talked and prayed. Just over her shoulder, on the mantle, was a huge gilt-framed portrait of the couple on their wedding day. They were astonishingly beautiful—like celebrities. Four years later, Tammy was still gorgeous, though she had gained some weight. When I asked her why her husband had left her, through her tears she repeated some of his last words to her: "You don't look like you did when I married you."

The night Tammy told me of her husband's shallow, spiteful comment, my thoughts immediately flew to another couple I know. A couple whose marriage, now more than 25 years strong, stands as a beautiful example of undying love.

What Real Love Looks Like

Kyle and Cheryl started dating in high school when he asked her to be his date for senior prom. Two years younger than he was, Cheryl was Kyle's first date. Kyle was Cheryl's. She was the only girl he had ever been interested in. She finished high school while he was away at college. One year after she graduated, they celebrated a summer wedding.

Kyle joined his father in business in their hometown, and the young couple bought a house next door to Cheryl's parents. They took to married life like old pros. She worked as a nurse's aide and kept up with a few friends. He played ball and hockey with the men's teams. Together they camped and fished, went to movies, and ate Chinese food at their favorite café. One year later, in the middle of the night, their future changed forever when Cheryl had a grand-mal seizure.

The tests began, and the diagnosis came in. Cheryl had a malignant brain tumor. It was inoperable. The neurosurgeon told Kyle that his wife had between two and five years to live. But he added, "I have one patient with a tumor like Cheryl's. She's still here. It's been 20 years." Kyle grasped that hope like a drowning man and held it.

The doctors recommended radiation and chemotherapy, as much as she could stand. Twice, Cheryl's hair fell out and returned. The first time it came back curly. The second time, it came back wispy and thin. She was taking so many drugs to control her ongoing seizures that Kyle had to keep track of them for her. It was all so confusing and very frightening. More tests confirmed that the tumor had shrunk and was not growing. But the seizures continued, so Cheryl was kept on a high dosage of potentially harmful drugs.

The years began to roll by. Cheryl stayed home, and Kyle arranged his work schedule so he was home for lunch every day. She always made his lunch—a tuna sandwich—by herself. It took her 30 minutes. After they ate, they played a hand or two of rummy before Kyle went back to work. He made supper when he got home around five. They ate together, watched their favorite television shows, and went to bed early.

More years passed. Eventually, as it got harder and harder for Cheryl to leave the house, Kyle stopped playing sports and fishing. He taught her how to use the computer, and she spent many happy hours playing solitaire and other simple games. He built her a tray on which to do puzzles, and she did hundreds of them. Kyle did all the shopping, even for his wife's clothes.

Years later it was discovered that Cheryl's cancer was completely gone. However, the residual scar tissue in her brain continued to require seizure-control drugs. These drugs changed her physically, emotionally, and behaviorally. She became forgetful and repeated herself. She had a hard time understanding plots in movies and books. She seldom cried but sometimes laughed inappropriately. She forgot the names of her nieces and nephews. And everything she did was at a snail's pace.

After 23 years, Kyle had to put Cheryl in the local nursing home after she fell and broke her hip trying to use the washroom. It was an excruciating decision. She did not want to go, but he could no longer care for her at home. He felt like a traitor. But he had no choice—the drugs had swollen her body to twice its normal size, and she needed the help of mechanical lifts and professional caregivers. Over the next few months Cheryl almost slipped away. Kyle thought he was losing her; he was despondent. She could not speak or move, was fed by tubes, and barely recognized him or her family. Every spare minute he had, he was at her side. Slowly she began to rally as her new home became more familiar.

A year later, she was up and around in a wheelchair, joking with the nurses and teasing the staff. She became the classic "teacher's pet" of the nursing home. Kyle no longer had to spoon-feed her, so they ate all their meals together in the dining hall with the other residents. After they ate, he pushed his wife back to her room or to the common room if she had visitors. Seldom sitting, he hovered near her chair. He would brush her wispy hair, gently caress her arms, and every few minutes, kiss her somewhere on her face. Always laughing at her silly comments—some the result of drug-induced confusion, some truly funny quips—Kyle brought sunshine into her world. Careful always to guard her dignity, he answered her every question, no matter how often repeated or how simplistic, with kind clarity and a smile. Cheryl knows she is loved with an undying love. And she is grateful.

∾ ∾ ∾

Kyle is one of my heroes. He is the best example I know "with skin on" of God's undying love. Cheryl isn't the girl he married, if you compare photos. But she's every bit the person he fell in love with on the inside. And he has never once forsaken his promise to love and to cherish, in sickness and in health. As God promised the Children of Israel, and us, the children of the new covenant, through His prophet Jeremiah, "I have loved you with an everlasting love; therefore, I have continued to extend faithful love to you" (31:3). Undying love. It is the kind of love that looks past our outward self and sees our inner beauty. Undying love does not abandon us in our season of need.

Even at Our Worst

When God found me in the wilderness, He asked me to do something risky. He asked me to tell the truth about my spiritual condition. Not just to family and friends, but publicly. As a matter of fact, this truth-telling was to be my personal message—and my gateway out of the wilderness. Like the Pharisee I had become, I had a reputation to protect. I had worn a mask for so many years that my unmasking would declare to the world that I had lived a lie. That I had been faking it. My image would be sullied.

In the risk God was asking me to take, that of tarnishing my image, He gave me an example to follow. His own. And He showed me His example in some of the men and women of the Bible. If ever there was a biblical character whose image took a beating, it must have been the prophet Hosea. His story is a parable of God's love for His chosen people, Israel. The book begins with this raw command:

> When the Lord first spoke to Hosea, He said this to him: Go and marry a promiscuous wife and [have] children of promiscuity, for the whole land has been promiscuous by abandoning the Lord (Hosea 1:2).

In Eugene Peterson's rendering in *The Message,* the wording offends my sensibilities but the meaning is abundantly clear:

> "Find a whore and marry her. Make this whore the mother of your children. And here's why: This whole country has become a whorehouse, unfaithful to me, GOD." Hosea did it. He picked Gomer daughter of Diblaim (Hosea 1:2-3 MSG).

In his commentary on Hosea, Peterson remarks, "It is an astonishing story: a prophet commanded to marry a common whore and have children with her. It is an even more astonishing message: God loves us in just this way—goes after us at our worst, keeps after us until he gets us, and makes lovers of men and women who know nothing of real love."[1] Peterson captures the essence of the message of this book in that last sentence. Because of God's undying love, it is His nature to pursue us.

Gomer bore Hosea three children before going back to her wild ways. Chapter 2 recounts the story of her wanton behavior and seductive dress. But God, the God who pursues, calls His child Israel back into relationship with Him through the story of Hosea reclaiming his wife. Here's His plan: "I'm going to start all over again. I'm taking her back out into the wilderness where we had our first date, and I'll court her" (2:14 MSG). This is what God will do for those of us who wander into the spiritual wilderness.

Just think about it. Where did God find us the first time we met Him face-to-face? Was it not in the wilderness? Is it not possible that God could find us there a second time, or a third or a fourth, should He so choose? What's so shocking to me is that He would lead us there and "speak tenderly to us" (verse 14). I don't know about you, but I learned as a kid that when I messed up, my parents led me into a "wilderness"—but not to talk tenderly to me. They usually spoke with their hands or a belt!

We know so little of real love today. Our minds and hearts are so dulled and battered with sarcastic sitcoms, trashy novels, the evening news, the morning paper, offensive movies, and the pornographic cyberbuffet that invades our homes via the Internet. We are seldom called upon to love as Hosea loved. To get our hands dirty in the life of the one we love; to lay down our life and keep our promises; to honor our vows even when our spouse breaks hers. Which of us would forsake our reputation, swallow our pride, debase our dignity, and go after a philandering spouse, as Hosea does in chapter 3? "Then God ordered me, 'Start all over: Love your wife again, your wife who's in bed with her latest boyfriend, your cheating wife. Love her the way I, God, love the Israelite people, even as they flirt and party with every god that takes their fancy'" (3:1 MSG).

"Hands-On" Passion

The words "start all over" leap off the page, bringing hope to the wanderer. When we have drifted far off course in our relationship with God, when months or years have passed wherein it seems God has been silent, we assume there's no going back. There can be no starting over. But God is in the recovery business. His love knows no end. He isn't afraid to get His hands dirty in the petty stuff of our lives. Even though we think He must grow weary of our wandering, He comes after us and calls us back.

God does not sit idly by while we wander, but as He calls, He also pursues, He forgives, He redeems (buys back), and He transforms. He uses everything in our lives, all our circumstances, to drive us back to Him. He sent His Son to live with us, die for us, and then live *inside* us. Talk about getting involved!

Where We Need It

Undying love is love that isn't worried about its image. Jim, a retired police officer, testifies that one of the reasons he is a believer today is because a Christian neighbor named Jesse met him on his turf, joining him in the pub one night when he was full of questions about God. Jesse didn't wait for a better time and place; he followed the lead of the Holy Spirit and went to the bar. How many evangelicals would take that risk in a town where the chances of running into someone they knew are relatively good? (I'm not sure I would.) Being seen going in or out of a "watering hole" would be damaging to our reputation. I'm not suggesting believers need to hang out in bars and look for opportunities to share their faith—but I am applauding the actions of a man who recklessly obeyed the Lord's bidding. Undying love doesn't stop at the door and consider its reputation; it meets us at our point of need.

A wanderer has forgotten—or maybe never knew—that God

loves us with such a hands-on passion that He isn't afraid to join us in our miserable and filthy condition. Mark Buchanan writes,

> Jesus got close enough to unholy people for the spark of holiness in Him to jump. He took the tax collectors, the rough fishermen, the harlots, the demon possessed, and gave back to them dignity and life….The Pharisees avoided these people lest they were infected with their sin and were overwhelmed by their evil.[2]

Finding the way out of the wilderness begins with a glimpse of God's undying love.

∽∽∽

When we begin to understand that God does still love us even though we've been wandering in a faraway land for a long time, we have just begun to understand the breadth of His love. When our spiritual sight returns, we realize there is no place we can go where His love cannot reach us. As that realization dawns, we start the journey of recovery. The warmth of His love draws us to Him. And we experience the beginning of what becomes, for a very long time, an overwhelming emotion and sensation—gratitude.

I am still in the deeply grateful stage of my returning to the Lord. Perhaps I always will be. I hope so. For I fear, if my gratitude begins to wane, it will indicate major slippage from resting in grace back toward spinning in the rodent wheel of works. When I was busy "earning" my salvation, I was never grateful. I was joyless, I was bitter; I was brimming with a sense of entitlement that would make the worst spoiled child look like Dickens' Tiny Tim by comparison. And the moment I lose that deep sense of gratitude is the moment I risk turning back toward the wilderness.

CHAPTER SEVEN

Come Out
with Your Hands Up

I urge you to present your bodies a living sacrifice.
The apostle Paul

Teachers open the door, but you enter by yourself.
Anonymous

$\mathcal{M}$y husband, Gerry, and I were in California in the late 1990s attending a meeting, and we took a drive down memory lane. The last stop on our pilgrimage would be an acreage near Modesto where we had lived more than a decade earlier. It had been covered with fruit trees of every kind. Delicious fresh fruit was available to us every day of the year. For people from a northern climate where fruit was scarce, small, and seasonal, this was paradise.

A six-foot-high chain-link fence enclosed the entire property, but another wooden fence divided the grassy area around the house from the orchard and outbuildings in the back half. The pickets of the fence were heavy with grapevines. The orchard produced everything from figs to kumquats. Pears, cherries, peaches, apricots, plums, apples, oranges, lemons, grapefruits—you name it, we had a tree for it. Beside the house was a rose garden that provided a fresh bouquet of vibrant color every week of the year. Wisteria vines covered the veranda, offering their heady fragrance in summer. It was idyllic; I spent hundreds of hours keeping the yard looking like something out of *Better Homes and Gardens*. We had many happy memories of our time spent there. This beautiful home was God's gift of love to us during the final two years Gerry was studying for his master's degree. Money was scarce, but we had all the fruit we could eat!

We drove from San Francisco to Modesto, reliving many events from our past as the miles rolled by. We arrived at the tiny rural settlement where the house was located and turned onto the street where we had once lived. But everything was different. We didn't recognize anything. What we recalled was not there. Thinking we were on the wrong street, we jogged one block over and tried again. Nope. The house wasn't there either. Eventually, after driving through the entire community, we returned to the street where we had begun.

Pulling up to the place where our old Eden should have been, we got out of the car, camera in hand. We had planned to take a photograph to show our teenage kids, who were too young to remember much of their years there. The property in front of us had no security fence. There was no vine-draped veranda. The rose garden was gone. The outbuildings were gone. There were no citrus trees in front of the house. No orchard out back. No grapevines. No lawn. There was neither tree nor grass nor anything green anywhere. What remained was a rundown house, badly in need of paint and a new roof. Where the veranda should have been was a sagging front stoop. The shabby house stood in the middle of an acre of dust so fine it was like mud-colored baby powder. We still could not believe this was the place we had once lived and thought we were mistaken until I saw something.

A little boy was sitting in the dust in front of the house,

watching us with vague interest. He was pushing a toy truck back and forth along an imaginary road. His truck had scraped away just enough dirt to reveal a small patch of pavement. What used to be the circular drive in front of the house was hidden under the powdery dust. I felt sick. This was the place all right, but it looked like it had been hit with a ten-year drought or a tornado or both. "Let's not take a picture," I said to my husband. "I don't want to remember it this way." He agreed, and we drove away, our day suddenly cloudy and dull. We didn't talk for a long time as we retraced our passage back through Silicon Valley and over the mountains towards the Bay area. We felt wounded.

$$\sim\sim\sim$$

The obvious message, that earthly investments do not last, is not what I am driving at here. As Christians we know that those who devote their lives to things temporal will leave this earth in spiritual poverty. Conversely, those who do their "gardening" in the souls of others will take their "fruit" with them. But God taught me something deeper through this experience. He gave me a glimpse into His Father heart.

What I was looking at as I scanned the wasteland in front of me that day could have been my spiritual life as seen through His eyes. Once lush and bursting with life and the promises of a good harvest in every season, it had been unwatered and untended for so long that everything had dried up. Like the branch disconnected from the Vine, life-giving nutrients could no longer flow to it (see John 15). The branch—the wanderer, that is—withered and fell away. All that remained under the dust of neglect was some foundational things that were barely even recognizable and not readily visible.

During my season of wandering, did God feel like I felt that day as I looked at all my work and tender care gone without a trace? Did His heart ache to see the waste? Did He mourn the loss of so much beauty? Did He feel heartsick and wounded? I think so. But I think He saw beyond that. There is another lesson.

> There is a difference between dead and dormant.
> Take heart, fellow wanderer—what seems like
> death is only a season of dormancy.

When my husband and I were finally able to talk about how such a complete transformation could have taken place, our best guess was that after we left, the new tenants must have stopped watering. In Modesto, where it does not rain for half the year, grapes, almonds, tomatoes, and a bounty of other produce are grown in abundance because of a system of canals that provide the needed moisture. Without irrigation, very little can survive the long summer drought. But the soil is so rich in nutrients that one can grow almost anything—as long as it gets water. We knew that within the dusty wasteland of our acreage was the potential for great abundance. We knew that the entire place could be restored to its former beauty.

God knew the same thing could happen to me in my wilderness by the addition of life-giving Water and the tender care of the Gardener's hands. The potential was all there—but barely visible. There is a difference between dead and dormant. Take heart, fellow wanderer—what seems like death is only a season of dormancy.

Waking—and Surrendering

Not everyone's journey of recovery will follow the same pattern. In my case, I awoke to the reality that God was pursuing me. I caught a glimpse of His undying, unconditional, grace-based love. That love drew me with its warmth, melting away my resistance. It was like a slow awakening, more akin to a tree coming out of its winter freeze and having the sap come up from the roots in response to the sun's warming rays than a bear coming out of hibernation. But both images get the idea across that what appears to be death is only a deep sleep. The natural outgrowth of recognizing His redemptive love was surrender. I quit running. By surrendering to His will instead of mine, I chose obedience. What I said *yes* to, what I agreed to do, became foundational in my recovery. But it went against everything I formerly believed. Before I explain more about surrender, let's take a look at Moses' life to gain some insight into the God who asks us to "come out with our hands up."

Wake Up and Listen

The book of Exodus tells the story of Moses being rescued from the waters of the Nile by Pharaoh's daughter. She raised him as her own. He was nursed by his Hebrew birth mother, though. She must have instilled in him the secret of his true heritage, because when he was a young man, he saw an Egyptian beating a Hebrew slave. This so enraged him that he killed the Egyptian and hid his body. However, news of the crime spread fast, and when Pharaoh got wind of it, he wanted Moses' head on a platter.

So Moses ran for his life. He never stopped until he was far enough away and in an obscure enough place that no Egyptian would bother to come looking for him. When he stopped running and sat down by a well, he was deep in the desert of Midian. Accustomed to having people listen when he spoke, since he was raised in the lap of luxury and influence, Moses saw another injustice. Again he stepped in to lend a hand. He helped seven sisters water their sheep by shooing away some pushy shepherds who didn't want to share the well with a bunch of girls. As a result,

Moses was welcomed by Jethro, a Midianite priest, shepherd, and father to the women he had aided. Jethro rewarded Moses with a place to live, a new job, and a family—by giving him his daughter Zipporah as a wife.

Like a chameleon, Moses kept changing colors. Born a Hebrew slave and raised an Egyptian nobleman, he then became a hot-headed murderer, a fugitive, a desert wanderer, and finally a shepherd and son-in-law to a Midianite. He got the surprise of his life when God encountered him in a way that was completely unprecedented and has never been repeated.

> Moses was shepherding the flock of his father-in-law Jethro, the priest of Midian. He led the flock to the far side of the wilderness and came to Horeb, the mountain of God. Then the Angel of the Lord appeared to him in a flame of fire within a bush. As Moses looked, he saw that the bush was on fire but was not consumed. So Moses thought: I must go over and look at this remarkable sight. Why isn't the bush burning up? (Exodus 3:1-3).

God had his attention. This was the way He worked in my life also. He woke me up. Once He had my attention, He asked me to do something completely new, something I could not do without His help.

Go Straight to Work from the Wilderness

> When the Lord saw that he had gone over to look, God called out to him from the bush, "Moses, Moses!"
> "Here I am," he answered.
> "Do not come closer," He said. "Take your sandals

off your feet, for the place where you are standing is holy ground." Then He continued, "I am the God of your father, the God of Abraham, the God of Isaac, and the God of Jacob." Moses hid his face because he was afraid to look at God (verses 4-6).

Moses may have been afraid to look at God because of his unworthiness. (More likely, he was afraid because tradition taught that no one could look upon God and live.) When God encountered me in my wilderness, I too reacted with fear. I was ashamed of my "wilderness estate" and felt unworthy.

Then the Lord said, "I have observed the misery of My people in Egypt, and have heard them crying out because of their oppressors, and I know about their sufferings. I have come down to rescue them from the power of the Egyptians and to bring them from that land to a good and spacious land, a land flowing with milk and honey...Therefore, go. I am sending you to Pharaoh so that you may lead My people, the Israelites, out of Egypt" (verses 7-8,10).

The people that Moses is supposed to lead just happen to be slaves. In other words, they're not exactly free to pick up and move. This is like trying to convince the leader of North Korea to allow all his subjects to flee to South Korea without a fight. As wild as this huge request is, this is not the point I want to take away from this passage.

The subtle but clear message of this scripture is that God calls Moses to His work straight from the wilderness. Moses doesn't hear, "Enroll in seminary. Work hard and get high marks. Cut your ministerial teeth serving as an associate pastor. Then go out and plant a church or two. Then go back for further study. Then publish a book about all you've learned. Then, when you've done all that, lead my people out of Egypt." God simply says, "Therefore, go. I am sending you." This is the point that took me a long time to understand because it went against the grain of what I had previously thought. As with Moses, God called me straight out of the wilderness into His business. He sent me out to speak in His name even before I fully understood the message I was called to preach.

A point of clarification is in order here. Although I had been experiencing spiritual drift for some time, I had been a believer for many years. During those years I had been actively involved in both learning and teaching God's Word. When God met me in my dry place and thrust me out to speak in His name, I was not completely ignorant or unqualified. I had a good deal of public-speaking experience as well as a decent amount of Bible knowledge in my background. I'm not suggesting that someone with no Christian training or spiritual preparation should leap into the spotlight. God did not send me into an operating theater to do neurosurgery without benefit of medical training. He reawakened my gifts and renewed my call.

Know That He Will Certainly Be with You

Neither was Moses unprepared for what God was asking. God saw beyond the obvious. Moses didn't, though. He asked God, "Who am I that I should go to Pharaoh and that I should bring the Israelites out of Egypt?" (3:11). Moses knows full well that when he checked out of Egypt on the red-eye flight, Pharoah wasn't too happy with him. God wants him to go ask a guy who already hates him to allow his unpaid labor force to leave? Who will build the pyramids? Not a good scenario! But beyond this, Moses knows the condition of his sinful heart. He is a murderer and a fugitive. He knows he has broken God's law and has wandered far from His presence. He is unworthy. This is classic wilderness thinking. *Who am I that God should commission me to speak out in His name? I'm a sinner. A wanderer. A transgressor. A fugitive from grace.*

But God answered Moses' question patiently: "I will certainly be with you" (verse 12). This simple phrase holds the key to wilderness recovery. God is telling Moses that he does not go alone or in his own strength. God Himself will be with him. In the same way, the Lord promises the wanderer that he does not walk alone. The journey to recovery is walked hand in hand. In my case, God put me in a place where I had to rely on Him. I came out of the wilderness by holding tightly onto the hand of my Guide. The sands of doubt and unbelief still blew around me like a Saharan dust storm, and the path was never clear. But as long as I held firmly to His hand, I walked toward wellness. Toward a mature faith. God's way of making sure I did not dare let go of His hand was to put me in a place I could not survive without Him. If I had continued to live my "comfortable" life I would have had little incentive for communion with Him.

This gives a whole new slant to the concept of surrender. Not only am I meekly laying down my defenses, spreading my arms wide, and saying, "Here am I," I am picking up His cross and carrying it from where I stand in the midst of swirling doubt and unbelief. I am saying, "Here am I, send me." Send me now. I agree there is no time to wait. I may not have too many seasons left, so send me now. Make my place of serving You also my training ground. Teach me on the job. Let me be your humble apprentice. Just don't let go of my hand!

Then Moses asked God, "If I go to the Israelites and say
to them: The God of your fathers has sent me to you,

and they ask me, 'What is His name?' what should I tell them?"

God replied to Moses, "I AM WHO I AM. This is what you are to say to the Israelites: I AM has sent me to you" (verses 13-14).

Moses realized he had two problems. Obviously, it was not going to be easy to convince Pharoah to let his slaves go. But added to that, Moses knew it would be even harder to get the Israelites to follow him. He had no established credibility with them. While they were living and working in horrible conditions—hungry, thirsty, sick, and exhausted—Moses had been sipping cordial out of golden goblets. How could he get them to trust him? The Lord told Moses to tell the truth, that their God had sent him. It was up to them whether or not they believed.

And that was His message to me as well. Like Moses I said, "I'm not worthy. I'm out here in this wilderness. I'm wandering in a land that worships false gods. I can't speak publicly in Your name. I have no credibility." But God said to me, "Therefore, go. And I will be with you." Added to that, He told me, "You are to say...'I AM sent you.'" For you, like for me, this means "I AM" will be with you all the way. He will be whatever you need—your strength, your wisdom, your courage. And that became my road to recovery. I surrendered to His call to go and tell the truth about my wilderness. And He walked with me, speaking "through" me and "to" me at the same time.

Why was Moses in the wilderness in the first place? Was it because of his impulsiveness in killing the Egyptian oppressor? Or was he exactly where God wanted him to be? Is it possible God used all of Moses' experiences—and even Moses' tendency toward rash behavior—to get him to the place he needed to be? Is it possible that the next assignment God had for Moses, the "really big shew" as Ed Sullivan used to say, would require a man with a mature faith? A faith forged in the wilderness? When God calls you out of your wilderness, He may hand you your biggest assignment to date. Will you surrender to Him?

The Lifestyle of Surrender

Trust is essential to surrender. Choosing to believe that God loves you is the first step in learning to trust Him. "Surrender is hard work. In our case, it is intense warfare against our self-centered nature," writes Rick Warren. He adds, "Surrendering is never a one-time event…There is a moment of surrender, and there is the practice of surrender, which is moment-by-moment and lifelong…It will often mean doing the opposite of what you feel like doing."[1] As we choose to surrender, over and over, we change the way we think.

In fact, surrendered thinking is the opposite of wilderness thinking:

- *Wilderness thinking says,* "Maybe there is no personal God. I haven't seen or heard from Him in a long time."

  Surrendered thinking says, "I choose to believe in the God I can't see or hear."

- *Wilderness thinking says,* "God can't love me, because I have wasted so much of my life in this wilderness of unbelief."

  Surrendered thinking says, "I choose to believe that the God who sent His Son to die in my place paid too dear a price to give up on me yet."

- *Wilderness thinking says,* "God will hold me accountable for my wasted potential, and I will never be who I could have been in Him."

Surrendered thinking says, "God is the one who orders my days—perhaps He has brought me through this experience in order to prepare me to do something for Him I never would have chosen on my own."

- *Wilderness thinking says,* "I am unfit to serve Him."

Surrendered thinking says, "God is in the recycling business, and He will send me out to help and encourage other wanderers, to point them to Christ and give them hope. Broken people love and serve broken people."

For every message of defeat that Satan sends into the heart of the recovering wanderer, there is a message of hope from God.

Surrender and Commitment Are Two Different Things

Much has already been said in Christian writing about the need for absolute surrender to God. Know this: Surrender and commitment are two different things. All during my wilderness journey, I was committed to God and to living a religious life. I was also dead, passionless, and without purpose. The Oxford Dictionary defines commitment as "obligation or pledge." Surrender, on the other hand, is defined as "to hand over, to give into another's power or control, especially under compulsion." When an army conquers opposing forces and the defeated side is forced to concede, they surrender. They come out with their hands up. That is what our loving Father is asking us to do. Put down our arms of religious activity, lay aside our shields of works-based religiosity, quit trying to be our own gods, and let Him be God in our lives.

Commitment means I am still in control, whereas surrender takes me out of the driver's seat. Commitment is, "Show me the array of choices, like a buffet table, and I will choose the ones that appeal to me." Surrender is, "Hand me a loaded plate and I'll try to eat it all!" Commitment is deciding on a plan. Surrender is going to God for His plan. Inherent in the act of surrender is submission to the Conqueror. We cannot surrender to God unless we submit ourselves to His absolute control. This means we no longer have a plan for our life. Instead we seek to understand His purpose for our existence.

This was a huge stumbling block for me as a new bride and wife of a young pastor. My nature is to be a biblical Martha—"so much to do, so little time, and good help is hard to find!" I am one of those to-do-list people. My lists were long and my nights were short. Problems arose when needs came knocking—often literally on my door—that weren't on my list. When I interrupted the flow of my day to meet needs and help people, my list got longer. Instead of moving some items to *tomorrow* or *never*, I would stay up later, work harder and faster, and still try to meet my goals. Not surprisingly, I was exhausted and unhappy most of the time. Not a great way to start a marriage—ask my husband!

My problem was that I was trying to please two masters—God and myself. I wanted to fulfill my own personal goals, career goals, and household goals, while God wanted me to know Him and to trust Him to guide me. He wanted me to surrender my precious to-do list to His control. I would not. Something had to give. I did. I burnt out. I started to "protect myself" from God. I put my hands over my ears and chanted "nananana" so I couldn't hear His voice. Like Moses, I said, "Please, Lord, send someone else" (Exodus 4:13 NCV). The Christian life was "too hard." God was a cruel taskmaster, and He wouldn't let me finish my vacuuming on schedule! And my journey into the wilderness commenced.

Surrender Is the Opposite of Self-Protection

The scene of Moses and God at the burning bush has one main plot thread: God tells Moses to go, that He will be with him all the way, and Moses keeps making excuses based on his inadequacies. "I am not a great man! How can I go to the king and lead the Israelites out of Egypt?" "What if the people say, 'What is [God's] name?' What should I tell them?" "What if the people of Israel do not believe me or listen to me? What if they say, 'The Lord did not appear to you'?" "Please, Lord, I have never been a skilled speaker." And finally, the classic wanderer's refrain: "Please, Lord, send someone else" (3:11,13; 4:1,10,13 NCV). John Ortberg says Moses' reply to God's call is, "Here am I, send Aaron."[2]

If God thinks Moses is capable, goes to all the trouble of holding an impromptu miraculous campfire just to get his attention, and then reassures him over and over that he can do it, why won't Moses believe Him? Because Moses is a wanderer. Wanderers are crippled by their failings. Paralyzed by fear. Bound by their past mistakes. When Moses tells God he is incapable, it's true. In his own strength, he can do nothing. But the whole point is, the Guy who lit the bush is offering to go with him! The wanderer is so accustomed to his self-protective stance of being afraid of God and disappointed by his own weakness that he often lacks the courage to surrender and say yes to God.

Moses crosses the line with his last excuse, and finally God gets fed up and agrees to let Aaron go along as his spokesman. I believe this contributes to the fact that Moses is never allowed to enter the Land of Promise. Wanderer, take heed—I don't know what the "magic number" is, but I do not think it's wise to make too many excuses. God has His limits. Is He calling you? Have you had a wake-up call?

The next several chapters in Exodus outline the plagues and pestilence God brought down on Pharoah's head before he was finally convinced to let the people go. He eventually relented and said, "Good riddance...for now." Moses won! Or did he? The children of Israel who left Egypt with Moses were a difficult, surly lot.

Moses had his hands full with their constant grumbling and childish desire to return to the bondage of Egypt just so that they could have more variety in their diet.

We are no different today than that dusty bunch of wanderers. More concerned with our earthly appetites than with submitting to God's leadership, we grumble and carp and try to convince Him we have a pretty good plan too. The result of all the Israelites' grumbling was that God kept them in the wilderness 40 years—until an entire generation had expired—and then He brought their children into the Land of Promise. Why were the Israelites kept out of the Promised Land? "They were unable to enter because of unbelief" (Hebrews 3:19).

That is the wanderer's sentence as well. We wander into the wilderness because of unbelief; we stop trusting Him and trust ourselves instead. As long as we continue in thinking our ways are better (or safer) than His, we will continue to wander. Self-protection is the opposite of surrender. Self-protection says, "I can't, I don't speak well, I haven't been trained, I've sinned, I'm unreliable, I've messed up before, I haven't memorized enough verses, I don't have a thing to wear!" And God keeps telling us, "I will be with you, I will give you the words, I will make a way." Will we believe Him? If we dare to surrender, He will lead us to freedom.

∽∽∽

I once taught an East Indian student in my grade-11 English class. Her name was Indira, and she was a delight. Even though English was her second language, she excelled. Experiencing the loneliness of culture shock and marginalizing bigotry, Indira did not find a personal friend for over a year. So I invited her to spend her spare time in the classroom with me if I wasn't teaching. Her being raised in a culture that reveres teachers automatically placed me on a pedestal in her eyes. The fact that I reached out to her in her friendless estate bumped me up a few more notches!

Indira invited Gerry and me to join her family for their Diwali celebration. Similar to Christmas, it is the big event of the year for Hindu families. When we went to her home, we discovered she was the youngest of a large family and her parents lived most of the year in India. But her oldest brother was an accountant in Canada and was raising his family as Canadian citizens, and she lived in his home. I asked Indira if she missed her parents during the long winters when they were in their homeland. She replied she did, but her brother was her guardian and he was good to her.

I asked her if East Indians still practiced arranged marriages. She told me that the brother with whom she lived had an arranged marriage. He had never met his wife until they were betrothed, and they had a strong, loving relationship. She talked about another brother of hers, who had "married for love"—and his marriage had not lasted. I asked her what she planned to do. "I will allow my brother to pick a husband for me," she replied without hesitation. Knowing that Indira was highly intelligent—she went on to study medicine, specializing in neurology—I questioned why she would leave this important decision in the hands of someone else. "I trust that my brother knows me and knows what would be best for me. I do not expect he would act without considering what would be in my best interests." This is surrender!

Indira is the only young woman I have known who has risked leaving the decision most people would call the biggest one of their life to another human. God expects no less from us. Absolute trust. Total submission. Complete surrender. Will we, like Indira, trust that He knows what's best for us and will not act outside our best interests? Until we do, we will remain in the wilderness.

CHAPTER EIGHT

Break the Conspiracy of Silence

When I kept silent, my bones became brittle
from my groaning all day long.
For day and night Your hand was heavy on me.
King David

If you do not tell the truth about yourself
you cannot tell it about other people.
Virginia Woolf

*W*hen my sister bought a house with a view, she got much more than she'd bargained for. Once the home was completed and her family was settled in, our family joined theirs for a potluck celebration. We arrived mid-afternoon and tramped from room to room oohing and aahing. The tour ended in the kitchen, where we stood, spellbound by the view.

The eating nook had huge windows on three sides. To the east we saw Calgary's Olympic Ski Jump 12 miles away. To the south, across the Bow Valley, wooded hillsides met the horizon. The river snaked along the valley floor and a train, like a toy, chuffed through the heart of the town. We watched as a golfer sank a long putt on the fifteenth green of the golf course just below. Turning west, we gazed in wonder at the towering, snowcapped Rockies. That view eclipsed everything we'd seen thus far. "This is our favorite view," my sister exclaimed. "It's a daily reminder of God's awesome hand."

"Who wants to play street hockey?" one of the boys hollered, breaking the reverie. Sons and dads stampeded for the door. My sister and I settled into the living room with a cup of tea while the three remaining girls set up a game on the kitchen table. Moments later the quiet was shattered by a scream from the kitchen. I catapulted from my seat.

"What is it? What's happened?" I demanded anxiously, arriving first on the scene. The girls were jumping up and down, waving their hands and shrieking. No one could speak; they pointed toward the west window. Wondering what could warrant such a commotion, I looked out. The mountains were intact. I turned back to the flapping females with a shrug.

"Not there, over there," my daughter said, shielding her eyes and pointing blindly. I looked again. This time I saw. My hand flew to my mouth, and I too was speechless.

"Will someone tell me what's going on?" my sister huffed, unable to see over my shoulder what I had seen—the cause of all the ruckus. Knowing that my sister was so modest that Queen Victoria was a wanton hussy by comparison, I hesitated to show her what had shocked us into silence.

It was in the new home of a just-moved-in neighbor, two lots away; there was no house yet on the empty lot separating us and the other home. Midway along the east wall of the neighbor's house was a floor-to-ceiling window of pebbled glass. This window, opaque when dry, became see-through when wet—on the inside. For some unknown reason, this neighbor had decided he liked plenty of natural light in his shower stall. The window brought in light, all right—but when wet, it revealed far more than the owner had probably intended. At that very moment, someone, facing away from us, was enjoying a shower on the other side of that all-betraying glass.

Unable to take the suspense any longer, my sister elbowed past me and looked west. At that instant, the bather turned in our direction. It was a man. Her gasp was all we heard before she snapped the cord that released the shade. It thwacked into position, blocking the western view. "This shade will stay down until we decide what to do," she harrumphed.

After everyone had calmed down, my sister and I resumed our places on the couch. By this time, our surprise had turned to sporadic bursts of embarrassed laughter, mixed with pitying tut-tuts for the unwitting neighbor. "Now I understand why you said that was your favorite view," I commented dryly. "You get to see *all* of God's creation." She put her head in her hands and groaned, knowing the teasing had only just begun.

"It's going to be really hard for me to meet this new neighbor with a straight face," my sister confided. "What am I supposed to say?"

"How about, 'Hello, I'm your neighbor—you don't know me but, boy, do I know you!' " I suggested tongue in cheek. More guilty giggling.

"Is it my Christian duty to tell them?" she asked. We tossed around a few possibilities. All were abandoned as too humiliating.

When the men came in, hot and sweaty from their game, their consensus was, "What kind of person puts a full-length window in his shower stall anyway? Maybe he wants an audience!"

My sister left her shade drawn for months and prayed for a solution. One day she called in great excitement. Work had commenced on a gigantic house on the empty lot between her and the unwitting exhibitionist. As the frame of the new building came together, we were all relieved to see it had no windows on the side that would have given them the view my sister was happy to give up. My sister raised her shade at last. "We can enjoy the mountains again!" she exclaimed.

"*Without* the Garden of Eden in between," I couldn't resist adding.

The Thin Glaze of Christianity

Believe it or not, this story holds a nugget of truth. The wanderer, if still in a religious community, often becomes a hypocrite. Unwilling to talk about the wilderness experience, he pretends all is well. He goes through the motions and hopes no one notices his superficial spirituality. But just like the man who thought he was enjoying a private shower, the wanderer reveals much more than he imagined.

> There is far more hope for recovery for the wanderer who remains connected...Far better to stay in church and break the conspiracy of silence by telling the truth about our spiritual condition.

Many wanderers are in denial. They would be offended if someone called them hypocrites. Wanderers find themselves living pretty much the same lives they lived prior to their conversions. This was something that greatly troubled me in my wilderness. I saw little variation between the religion I had practiced as an unbeliever and the religion I practiced 25 years later as a "numbbeliever." It felt like I had come full circle and the trail was littered with broken hearts. The "thin glaze of Christianity,"[1] as Ray Stedman calls it, that covered my life was riddled with cracks, threatening to shatter and fall off completely before I could find my way out of the wilderness. That thin glaze is like the window in the shower stall; it reveals as much as it hides.

I've seen it in people's eyes. That hard glint of darkness hooded by a patina of religious duty. I've had that look myself, which is probably why I can recognize it in others. Those who leave the church are, in a way, only trying to live more honestly—without hypocrisy—than wanderers who remain and fake it. But there is far more hope for recovery for the wanderer who remains connected to the Christian community than for those who walk away. Far better to stay in church and break the conspiracy of silence by telling the truth about our spiritual condition to even one trusted friend…than to walk away and tell no one. Of all the people I know who have encountered a season of dryness and left the church, none of them have returned. Not one. Not so far. However, for people like me who endure even an extended period of wilderness, staying involved with other believers has been a vital, life-restoring connection.

Risk Telling the Truth

A wanderer who wants to have any hope of recovery must break the conspiracy of silence about his spiritual condition. It's a risk, but it's worth the taking. I admire the candor and courage of George Mueller, who wrote, "There was a day when I died, utterly died, to George Mueller and his opinions, preferences, tastes and will; died to the world, its approval or censure; died to the approval or blame of even my own brethren and friends; and since then I have studied only to show myself approved unto God."[2] This is the attitude we need, fellow wanderer. Forsaking our pride and choosing to be honest before God and others, we must risk telling the truth about ourselves. A mature faith is one that "studies to show itself approved unto God." It is the sound of God's applause that we seek in our quest for a grown-up faith.

Follow the Spirit's Lead

Do not discount the role of the Holy Spirit in this process. I was peeling potatoes late one afternoon, gazing mindlessly out my kitchen window, when into my mind came the name of someone dear to me who lives in another province. I began to pray for her. Then came the sense that I should go visit her. Fortunately, I acted on that holy impulse and went to the telephone. I called some others who also knew and loved her, and together we planned the trip. Then I called my friend and asked if she would host us. She agreed, sounding excited.

Three of us made the drive to visit her and spent a wonderful relaxing weekend talking, laughing, eating too much—the usual. The night before we left, my friend and I went out for an after-dinner stroll. We hadn't gone far when she told me something she had kept secret for decades: "I am struggling with clinical depression and am seeing a psychiatrist." This may not seem like a big deal to some readers, but for my friend, it was a hard admission to make. She went on to say that our trip to visit her that weekend must have been inspired by the Holy Spirit because she knew she needed to "come out of the closet"—but she did not want to do it via telephone or e-mail. It needed to be face-to-face.

It is now several years since my friend broke the conspiracy of silence about her struggle with debilitating depression. She looks back to that experience of "going public" as an important turning point in her journey of recovery. And we both acknowledge that the Spirit's influence was key in making that confession possible.

Admit You Are a Wanderer

The fifth step in the 12-step recovery program of Alcoholics Anonymous is this: Alcoholics "admitted to God, to ourselves, and to another human being, the exact NATURE of our wrongs."

Clarence H. Snyder, one of the original members, interprets it this way:

> We put ourselves on record and leave no options or reservations! Note that it states, NATURE of our wrongs—not the wrongs themselves! We are not required to narrate details of our many indiscretions. Many of them we don't even remember, nor are conscious of. This is not a laundry for dirty linen; this is recognition of character defects, which need elimination or adjustments![3]

Snyder's interpretation captures the idea of what I mean when I use the term truth-telling. It's not that we go around giving everyone intimate glimpses into the "shower stalls" of our lives—rather, we admit to a trusted friend that we struggle with doubt and unbelief and that we are in a period of dryness in our relationship with God. Did you notice I said, we *are in* a period of wilderness? We admit that *right now*—not last year or last month, but today—we are struggling.

When a wanderer admits that God seems distant, that spiritual passion has seriously waned, perhaps even died, and that nothing done thus far has made any difference, this is a crucial step toward recovery. If that is where you are right now, do not give up. It means you are on the right road, the road that will eventually lead you out of the wilderness of dry faith. Have you told anyone yet? Don't delay.

Many evangelical churches offer what's known as an altar call for people who appreciate an opportunity to publicly confess a need or tell of a decision God has brought to mind. "Going public" adds the dimension of accountability—someone else now knows what you have decided. My church practices this custom, and I have responded many times over the years by going forward to pray and confess and to pray with others. Confession is good for the soul, most people agree, even the irreligious. When we admit our need, we have already begun to recover. It's worth repeating: "Therefore confess your sins to each other and pray for each other so that you may be healed" (James 5:16 NIV).

Why the Secrecy?

Here is the $64,000 question: Why is there a conspiracy of silence? Why are wanderers unable or unwilling to admit publicly the condition of their heart? Why do we feel ashamed or embarrassed about our season of dryness? Perhaps the biggest reason is because evangelical Christians believe what the Scriptures say about the "born again" experience being necessary for salvation. It's how we become Christians. After our spiritual rebirth, we have the Holy Spirit alive in us. We are different. Different from what? From the "sinner" we were prior to our conversion. And that is where we can run into problems. We take this truth in the wrong way and think we're not going to sin anymore.

When we are converted, God gives us a new heart, and He implants the living Holy Spirit within us as our guide. He readily forgives every sin, confessed or otherwise, and sets our feet on a new path. And our new life begins. A life of faith. But our new life is saddled with something—our old "body of death," as the apostle Paul calls it. And that old body, called "the flesh" in Scripture, is stuck in some ruts. Habits—what we like to call baggage—ride with us into our new relationship with God. Just like the divorced man who marries again carries baggage from his failed relationship into the new one, so do we carry old habits, hurts, and hates into our new life with Christ.

The Bible teaches that Christians do sin:

If we say, "We have no sin," we are deceiving ourselves, and the truth is not in us. If we confess our sins, He is faithful and righteous to forgive us our sins and to cleanse us from all unrighteousness. If we say, "We have not sinned," we make Him a liar, and His word is not in us (1 John 1:8-10).

We will continue to sin as long as we live on earth. However, people like me who experienced a radical conversion whereby we saw extreme changes in our lifestyles tend to try to discern a trend. The trend I saw began with a large spike on the graph the day I prayed and asked Jesus to take control of my life. Huge changes were immediately evident in my behavior, language, and lifestyle. This continued fairly steadily for several years. As any trend-watcher will tell you, an upward trend augurs continued positive movement. In other words, the "better" I got, the more I assumed I would continue until I achieved the "sinless" life…or something very near it.

So what do you do with the inescapable reality of a wilderness experience in a life that was headed for "sinless perfection"? Suddenly the stats don't look so good. The graph has taken a dip, and then a dive, and then bottomed out. No corporate executive likes to bring those kinds of stats to the quarterly report meetings. Neither do Christians like to advertise that they seem to be "in a slump." And so we do what some famous—now infamous—companies have done in order to cover up the downward trend. We cook the books. We hide the truth. We lie. We throw on our power suits, order a limo, and glide into our corporate meetings with an armload of "fixed data." That pretty much describes me as I attended church Sunday after Sunday as a wanderer.

There are dozens of scriptures that declare we are no longer slaves to sin—that sin no longer rules us but we are slaves to God.

Romans chapters 6 through 8 go into great detail on the subject of sin. Their writer, Paul, knew better than anyone what Jesus and the Hebrew Scriptures taught about sin. However, Paul was human. He admittedly sinned and it caused him as much frustration as it causes us. Here's how he explains the tension between Jesus' command that we be sinless and the reality of sin in the Christian's life:

> We know that the law is spiritual; but I am made out of flesh, sold into sin's power. For I do not understand what I am doing, because I do not practice what I want to do, but I do what I hate. And if I do what I do not want to do, I agree with the law that it is good. So now I am no longer the one doing it, but it is sin living in me. For I know that nothing good lives in me, that is, in my flesh. For the desire to do what is good is with me, but there is no ability to do it. For I do not do the good that I want to do, but I practice the evil that I do not want to do (Romans 7:13-19).

Although Christ gives us a brand-new heart when we are born again, that heart is in a body that has some deeply entrenched patterns. Satan and the flesh conspire against us as we strive to be all that we can be in Christ.

It's Painful to Admit

If each of us began to be honest with ourselves, with God, and with others, our church would instantly become a better place. It would become a place where people inside, as well as those looking in from the outside, would not be living under an illusion. Instead, our churches are sometimes too similar to the man behind the see-through glass. Thinking our sins are hidden, glossed over by tidy coifs and trendy suits, we go in on Sunday morning and come out unchanged. Untouched by the God of miracles we lustily sing about. Unaffected by His call on our lives. Unmoved by His challenge to be like Him. Unresponsive to His invitation to meet Him in a quiet place.

Why the conspiracy of silence? Because Christians don't like to admit they sin. What does Scripture say? "If we say, 'We have no sin,' we are deceiving ourselves." It's just not easy to admit we are a wanderer. Just last night I attended a party with many others I've worked with in the past. When asked what was keeping me busy these days, I said I was working on a book about the spiritual wilderness. When asked why I chose that topic I explained I'd experienced a long drought in my faith and the Lord had called me back into relationship with Him. The next question, not surprisingly, was, "When did this occur? Did I know you then?"

Throwing caution to the wind, I decided to be truthful and said the wilderness was quite recent. "I may still be in it," I continued. If I could have captured on film the looks on the faces around me, I would not have to say another word about why wanderers keep quiet and don't risk breaking the conspiracy of silence. I have to wonder, is it because so many of us struggle with doubt that the subject of unbelief is so threatening? Is it that, if we don't talk about it, perhaps we won't have to admit it's real? I went on and filled them in: "I feel as though God has brought me such a long way from where He found me deep in the wilderness. But each year that passes I look back on the year before and see how far I've come, so the journey continues. Maybe I'm not in the wilderness anymore—but the life I now live is like one long road to recovery."

Even though I was tempted to gloss over the truth and talk about the wilderness like it was all wrapped with a tidy bow and put on the shelf years ago, I knew God had called me to be honest. The reaction I received was not unusual or even unexpected, but it affected me. I want to be liked. I want people to respect me. Their reaction didn't encourage me to continue being confessional. If anything, my mind screamed, *Keep quiet, you fool! Can't you see they don't want to hear this?*

Will I Ever Reach Mature Faith?

The journey to recovery may be all I'll ever get. Maybe, like Moses, I'll never make it to the Promised Land. But guess what? It's not about me or what I want. It's about Him and His purposes. And the road to mature faith sure feels a lot more promising than the wilderness, and I'm grateful for that. He has called me to tell the truth about my wilderness and so I'm doing it. I may never achieve the depth of intimacy I hear about and read about from my heroes in the faith. I hope I do. I am pressing on "in faith" that I will grow to know Him more. But there are no guarantees. Does that mean I quit? Not a chance. After God woke me up to how far I had drifted, I risked being obedient. I said *yes* to His request for me to speak the truth. Every day is still a risk. Every day I still have to choose to trust the invisible God and relinquish "self" control.

Remember how grown up we all thought we were at 18? I was ready for anything and well able to handle it like an adult, I thought. What a joke! I'm still learning simple life lessons—and I'm in the forgetting-pots-on-the-stove stage of life! For that reason, I hesitate to say I've reached mature faith. Because each year I look back I see how much I've learned and grown and how much my walk with the Lord has improved. The only way I can say I've achieved mature faith is to define maturity as a period of continued growth.

ᏁᏁᏁᏁ

I expect the churches most of you attend are similar in that many who claim pew space on Sunday morning are people like me who struggle with doubt and unbelief. Some of them know it and are uncomfortable with it. Some of them think it's normal because they've never known any different. And some are in denial. "What's wrong with my Christianity?" they ask. "I'm like everybody else." And, sadly, they are.

Where do you get the courage to break the conspiracy of silence? You get the courage from knowing who God is and what He is doing in your life. You've experienced a wake-up call. You realize your false god is no longer adequate. You recognize that God is pursuing you. God wants to extend His grace to you—as with the prodigal son, He wants you to come home. You must take the first step of trust, like Peter, and "get out of the boat." This is surrender. This is real faith.

Therefore, you must realize there is no shame in being a wanderer. God will use your wilderness to forge a faith that works in the real world. This is a genuine Christian experience. There is no need to be ashamed of God's activity in your life, even if it takes place in a desert. When we became a follower of Christ, we were under no illusion that we deserved Him. We must have the same attitude of utter dependence on His grace that we began with. Yes, we start our walk of faith with grace, but how quickly this grace walk is transformed into a religion of works! We are embarrassed to acknowledge our wilderness journey because it doesn't give us any credits in a works-based economy. But if we're honest, we still desperately need Christ and deserve nothing from Him in return—just like at our moment of conversion. Why not admit it?

Dare to break the conspiracy of silence by admitting to others that you sometimes wrestle with unbelief. If you get a stunned reaction, simply explain that without doubt there can be no faith. Remember what faith is: It's Peter stepping out of the boat onto a liquid surface that he knows will not hold him up unless Jesus is in control. Anyone who doesn't have a moment of doubt as they consider stepping out onto water is too stupid to be fishing in the first place! Saying *yes* to Jesus in the midst of doubt is mature faith.

CHAPTER NINE

Reckless Obedience

Therefore, go.
God speaking to Moses

If you debate for a second when God has spoken, it is all up.
Oswald Chambers

*B*ecca was still young in her faith when God asked her to do something she thought was sheer lunacy. She could hardly believe or understand the reasoning behind this request, and so she sought wise counsel from her spiritual mentor, Karla, also her best friend for a decade. Becca told her friend what she thought God was asking her to do. She added that He had also given her a promise from Scripture: "I know the plans I have for you...plans for [your] welfare, not for disaster, to give you a future and a hope" (Jeremiah 29:11). Karla had learned not to second-guess God so, with some trepidation, she advised Becca to obey without delay.

∽∽∽

Becca is attractive and intelligent, but she has always battled low self-esteem. She chalks it up to a date rape in her early teens—

an event about which she kept silent, wrongly assuming it must
have been her fault. In her confusion and repressed pain, she fell
into the habit of living two lives. During the week she was an hon-
ors student. But on weekends, another person emerged from
some wounded place deep inside. What did she have to lose, she
sadly concluded, since she was already soiled? She went looking
for comfort in the arms of her boyfriends. Those interludes only
added to her burden of shame and her poor self-image.

In her late teens, Becca met Gil. A whirlwind romance that
included trips to exotic resorts made her feel prized and desirable.
They had a huge wedding three days before her twentieth birthday; she was happy, in love, and determined to make a new start.

Gil, more than ten years her senior, wanted kids right away.
After the second child, the realities of life in the Mommy
Trenches—colicky babies, diapers, dishes, laundry—took their toll
on Becca's body and emotions, and she grew listless. Many days she
couldn't even get out of bed to care for her young family because
depression totally sapped her strength. Her life seemed so mun-
dane, and the needs of her children overwhelmed her. Although
Gil truly loved her, he was busy climbing the corporate ladder during the week and devoting most weekends to being an outdoors-
man. Becca was tired all the time, lonely, and emotionally drained.
She needed a change, she thought. Believing that a happy mommy
is a better mommy, she placed her youngest child in day care—the
older boy was already in school—and found a part-time job doing
office work.

Within a year, Becca had slipped back into old thinking habits.
Even though she loved her husband, she again tried to fill her
wounded emptiness in the arms of other men. Over the next
decade, she had two brief extramarital relationships. Inevitably,
after each affair Gil would find out and threaten to leave, but

promising to change, she would ask for another chance, and he always relented for the sake of the children and his love for her.

However, there was a limit to Gil's forgiving heart, and he reached that limit after the third fling. He warned Becca that the next time would be the last. And he meant it. Becca was careful for a very long time. Sadly, she and her husband did not make any changes to their lifestyle. He still worked 12-hour days; she spent her best hours at the office and, like too many women, did the second shift at home. Sure enough, she again grew despondent. She allowed the guilt of her past mistakes to convince her she was worthless, and before long she slipped into another relationship. As always, she was looking for someone or something to make her feel cherished—in an effort to fill the gaping hole in her heart. As with the others, the relationship quickly soured. And instead of filling her emptiness it added crippling weight to her emotional baggage.

But this time, Gil didn't find out. After the illicit relationship ended, Becca felt so devastated by her inability to keep promises and honor her marriage vows that she had a complete breakdown. Gil was fed up. Adding housework and child care to his already crowded schedule filled him with resentment, and he withdrew emotionally. The "D"-word was thrown around in some of their late-night spats. Gil moved into the guest room and began looking for an apartment. Now Becca felt completely alone, without anyone to hold her and convince her, if even for an hour, that she mattered.

Unable to get out of bed many days, Becca lost her job. During this time, her friend Karla kept tabs on her. The peace so evident in Karla made Becca's emptiness by contrast seem that much bleaker. On a particularly hard day, she surprised Karla by asking point-blank what made her so different. Karla described her own search for meaning that had left a trail of devastation, and how she had given her life to God. When Becca asked her if that was available to her also or if she was too far gone, Karla gently led her to the cross of Christ for forgiveness and new life.

Becca's conversion made such an impact that her entire family, including Gil, followed suit within two years. Husband and wife found an intimacy they never dreamed possible as Christ's love brought healing. As their marriage deepened, they dreamed about working together to help other couples. The future looked good.

༄ ༄ ༄

Then the bomb dropped. In the midst of this shining time, God whispered in Becca's ear, *Tell Gil about that last affair.* She was speechless with horror. Why now, after all this time? Why sink the ship that had finally found safe harbor? She couldn't believe her spiritual ears. The Holy Spirit nudged her: *You can never know true intimacy until you have complete honesty. Just do it.*

Eager to obey before she lost her nerve, she told her husband the truth that night after the kids were in bed. He went nuts. Throwing things, yelling, calling her unspeakable names, he left the house in a rage. Becca was numb with shock; she was beyond consoling. Why would God do this to her? Had she not heard Him correctly? Had she not checked with her mentor and gotten her blessing? She was thrown into a panic of doubt and despair, and the old enemy of self-hatred almost swallowed her up. She called out to God for answers, but heard nothing—Gil's response had shaken her confidence in her ability to hear the Father's voice. His promise of a "future and a hope" seemed remote.

Over the next several weeks, things went from bad to worse as Gil continued to rage and hurl insults and accuse his wife of trying to destroy him. The weeks turned into months; their bedroom became a battle zone. Gil moved to the guest room once more.

The days passed in silence as they refused to fight in front of their sons—but late at night, the weapons came out. After several months of warring with words, Becca was losing the fight on two fronts: Her husband's sense of betrayal was unchanged and her old nemesis—crippling insecurity—had her emotionally flattened and spiritually empty.

She wept a river of tears, begged forgiveness a thousand times, and promised to do whatever it took to rebuild his trust in her, but Gil refused to reconcile. Unable to think of anything else to say or any way to make it up to him, Becca gave up hope and grew silent. The next time he flew into a fit of yelling, she interrupted his rant by calmly saying, "I've done and said everything there is to say to make it better. There's nothing more I can do. Now it's up to you. Either you forgive me and we move on—or you don't and we end it." Slumped in a chair, pale and shaken, she had no more tears to cry.

Gil dropped his hands to his sides. Deflated and speechless, he left the house and drove aimlessly for hours. When he returned, in a calmness that comes only from God, he went to his wife and forgave her. "I felt so assaulted as a man," he cried. "Because I had vowed the next affair would be the last, I felt that if I didn't follow through, I would lose my self-respect. I can see now that Satan used that lie to destroy both of us."

Tenderly, through many shared tears, Gil and Becca began a journey of forgiveness and hope. Now they say that their marriage could not possibly be better. They say that the horror of those months of strife was worth it because of the depth of their new love. They could not be where they are today if they had not walked through the wilderness of near-marital-death together. Complete honesty led to true intimacy. The path was rough, often dark and dangerous, but the end was assured because He who promises is faithful.

If you hear the voice of God, take the advice of Oswald Chambers:

> If you debate for a second when God has spoken, it is all up. Never begin to say—*Well, I wonder if He did speak?* Be reckless immediately, fling it all out on Him. You do not know when His voice will come, but whenever the realization of God comes in the faintest way imaginable, recklessly abandon. It is only by abandon that you recognize Him. You will only realize His voice more clearly by recklessness.[1]

A word of caution is in order, though. The first thing Becca did after hearing the Lord's command was to go to her spiritual advisor and ask her advice. If you believe God is asking you to do something "off the wall," check it out first. Go to your pastor or a trusted spiritual mentor and lay the whole thing out for them. Pray together. Go to the Scripture and ask God to speak clearly through His Word. Becca heard from the Lord, was given a scriptural promise, checked it out with her spiritual adviser, and then recklessly obeyed.

Assume God Is Still Speaking

Depending on how long you have been in the wilderness, you may no longer recognize the sound of God's voice. Or maybe you've never been sure if what you are hearing is His instruction or your own ideas. A good place to start, as John Eldredge says, is to "begin by assuming that God is still speaking."[2] The wanderer chooses, sometimes a dozen times an hour, to believe that even though he cannot see or hear God, He is there. Reckless obedience is taking the risk that the "voice" just might be His, and then acting on it.

How is this "acting on it" different from being a hypocrite who fakes faith? The main difference is the heart. The motivation of the faker is the desire to remain hidden, pretending to be righteous and hoping no one will know his spirit is dry. The recovering wanderer who is "acting like a believer" is choosing, on faith, to believe what he reads in the Word and follow what may be the nudging of the Holy Spirit in the quest for a relationship with the living God. This is a risky venture. "If you are not pursuing a dangerous quest with your life, well then, you don't need a Guide."[3] But you do not walk alone; the indwelling Holy Spirit is in lockstep with you. When you as a recovering wanderer sense, even for a moment, that the Spirit is speaking—then, on faith, follow!

When you choose to believe, even in your weakened spiritual state, that God still speaks, you are like the man who came to Jesus for his son's healing and cried out, "I do believe! Help my unbelief" (Mark 9:24). That, in a phrase, is the prayer of the recovering wanderer. Reckless obedience means that in the face of our own overwhelming skepticism, we step out on faith. Like Becca, sometimes we step into a storm that threatens to swallow us up, for "obedience is no guarantee of being spared adversity."[4]

Daring to Get Out of the Boat

Out on the Sea of Galilee in the middle of the night, having left Jesus behind on shore at His own request, Peter and the disciples are caught in a vicious storm. Fighting to stay afloat, they do not recognize Jesus as He approaches, walking on the water. They are terrified of what seems to be a ghostly apparition. Jesus identifies Himself to reassure them. In the narrative we mentioned briefly in the previous chapter, Peter then decides to check and see if it really is Jesus coming across the waves: "Lord, if it's You...command me to come to You on the water" (Matthew 14:28). John Ortberg believes this story illustrates both risk-taking and obedience in equal portions. By asking Jesus to "command" him to come toward Him over the waters, Peter was demonstrating his absolute trust in Christ. He was willing to step out, literally, in faith. As Ortberg says in his book of the same name, "If you want to walk on the water, you've got to get out of the boat."[5]

Ortberg continues, "I believe there is something—Someone—inside us who tells us there is more to life than sitting in the boat....So let me ask you a very important question: What's your boat?"[6] He defines our "boat" as whatever we put our trust in. The wanderer, instead of trusting in God, has decided on self-trust. Unless we surrender and allow God free rein in our life, we're "up the creek without a paddle." Stuck in the boat...lost in the wilderness...they're one and the same.

And the Blind Shall Lead Us...

If this challenge to "walk by faith" when faith seems scarce frightens you, take heart from the biblical account we talked about in chapter 3. When Jesus heals the man born blind, He does so on the Jewish Sabbath. Making a paste from clay and spittle, Jesus applies it to the blind man's eyes and tells him to go wash in the pool of Siloam. The blind man, exercising his faith, somehow finds his sightless way to the pool and washes his eyes. Perhaps you think the guy had nothing better to do? "Why not stumble off and grope your way to a pool? It beats sitting here in the hot sun all day begging for pennies!" Those are the cynical thoughts of a wanderer. That, my friend, is wilderness thinking. Choose instead to rejoice that this man, who has been blind from birth, recklessly abandoned his begging post and, in faith, did as he was told.

First-century Jews believed that when calamity befell a person or household, it was a direct result of that person's sin or his parents'. Therefore the blind man or his parents must be sinners, worthy of punishment. Suddenly the Jews were confronted with a miraculously healed man and this messed up their theology. Not knowing how to solve this in their minds, they marched the formerly blind man to see the Pharisees and put the question to them. A second complication in this story is that Jesus did this healing on the Sabbath. According to rabbinic law, healing was work and was thus forbidden on the Sabbath.

The Pharisees were split in their opinion of this event. Some thought Jesus was of the devil—a sinner and an imposter for breaking Sabbath law. Others mused that bad people cannot perform good works, so Jesus must be from God. The healed man grew weary of the inquisition. Why was something so simple made so complex? He mocked the Pharisees: "I've told you over and over and you haven't listened. Why do you want to hear it again? Are you so eager to become his disciples?" (John 9:27 MSG). This was like throwing fat on the fire. The Pharisees exploded with indignation, claiming they were followers of Moses, to whom God had clearly spoken—but in regard to "this man," Jesus, they did not trust or believe Him or know where He came from.

> Jesus blesses us. He commends our efforts to believe, understanding how hard it is to place our trust in something we cannot see or touch. He's on our team.

The response to this miracle reveals a certain principle of faith: "Although faith may produce miracles, miracles do not necessarily produce faith."[7] Confronted with irrefutable visual evidence as well as verifiable sound testimony, people refused to believe Jesus was God in the flesh, Messiah. We wanderers, some 20 centuries hence, are asked to base our belief on only the written record of the event. Don't be too hard on yourself if doubt nibbles at the edges of your mind. Even those who saw did not believe. Jesus gently rebukes His disciple Thomas, who refused to believe until he had seen the risen Christ for himself and verified His identity by touching His mortal wounds: "Because you have seen Me, have you believed? Blessed are they who did not see, and yet believed" (John 20:29 NASB). We are in the "did not see" time in history. Jesus blesses us. He commends our efforts to believe, understanding how hard it is to place our trust in something we cannot see or touch. He's on our team.

In my early days of faith, I childishly assumed it would have been so much easier if I had lived in Palestine at the time of Christ. *If I would have seen Him heal and heard Him preach, I would have followed,* I thought. And perhaps, looking back now through the haze of the intervening wilderness, if I had lived in Palestine as a young woman, I would have followed Him. As an 18-year-old college student, I had no trouble abandoning my past life, religious tradition, and former friends to follow Christ.

But I am sure, to my shame, that if I had lived in Palestine during my wilderness season, I would have joined the Pharisees in condemning Jesus for breaking religious laws. As a faker and pretender all those years, keeping the rules became terribly important to me because that's all there was! Rule-keeping was how I measured my relationship with the God I no longer experienced. Even though I was blind to His activity, I felt some false security in the fact I was still "doing all the right things." And, just like the first-century Jew, I judged the evidence of His favor by how things looked in my outward life. If things were calm at home and the kids were doing well at school and my husband was enjoying his work and the bills were getting paid on time, I assumed God was rewarding me for "faithful service." If things went awry, I immediately wondered, *Who has sinned? Me or someone in my family?*

ᘓᘓᘓ

"It's easy for us to move from an intimate relationship to religious activity," said Henry Blackaby when he preached at my church recently. "We are better at activity than relationship." Ask yourself, *Am I practicing religion or am I in a relationship with Jesus? Am I experiencing the presence of God in my life?* Jesus promises His disciples in John 14 that God will send them a Helper once He is no longer with them. The moment we believe, the Holy Spirit takes up residence in our life. If I am not experiencing the presence of God in my life, Blackaby said, then I must call upon the Holy Spirit. How do I do that? "Just do it!" he said. "You are one prayer away from allowing the Spirit of God free rein. You are one prayer away from experiencing what God has promised."[8]

CHAPTER TEN

Full of Grace

The law was given through Moses;
grace and truth came through Jesus Christ.
The apostle John

I do not understand the mystery of grace—
only that it meets us where we are,
but does not leave us where it found us.
Anne Lamott

ONCE UPON A TIME there lived a young woman. You wouldn't call her beautiful, but she was not unpleasant to behold. She did, however, have one unique characteristic. One thing she was sure everyone had noticed—and yet no one commented on it. Her backpack. She had carried her backpack for as long as she could remember. At night she would lay it beside her bed, and in the morning she would strap it back on before doing anything else.

She couldn't remember when she had first picked it up. She never knew who had given it to her, or when—she had always had it. Like a birthmark. She never thought about leaving it beside the bed in the morning. She never took a day off from carrying it. It was a compulsion, a need; she was driven to pick it up. And she always did.

It never occurred to her that others might not carry a backpack.

She assumed that, like hers, it was underneath their clothes and didn't show. *Everyone has a backpack,* she told herself, *it's just that no one talks about it.* And so each morning she thought, *This is my load to bear.*

∾ ∾ ∾

But as years went by, it got harder for her to carry. She reasoned that was because of what was in it. Every day she added to it. She couldn't remember if it had ever been empty. She had been doing this for so long, she did it without thinking. Although it never seemed to get full, it felt heavier every morning. It never showed through her clothes either—although it did seem to her that it should, considering its bulk.

Although her backpack had never been empty, she could remember a time it had seemed lighter—when she had been meeting with The Father. The land was divided about The Father; some loved Him with all their heart and wanted to be His children. But others hated Him and wanted nothing to do with Him, or with those who loved Him. She remembered the first time she'd met The Father. Her dad explained what He could mean to her life. She was nine years old. She asked her dad if she could meet The Father. He took her hands in his and introduced her right then and there. She was amazed at the peace she sensed. At how the way she thought and felt changed.

But that was years ago. It seemed like a story from a book she had once read. It had been years since she'd felt freedom or peace. The Father had been faithful to her; there were times she heard Him calling. But it was in spite of her and not out of her willingness to be near Him. She knew that The Father had blessed her along the way. He had taught her things about Himself. She tried to drop by His house, but it seemed as though she could only get so close. She knew why. It was because of the backpack.

She cared for her backpack as if it were a treasure. When its seams ripped from the weight or the zipper broke from all the opening and shutting, she would fix it, making it stronger. And then she would squeeze more in. Some days it was harder to carry than others. Some days she felt weaker and less able to lift the weight, but she couldn't leave it at home. It was her backpack, her burden. Her purpose in life was to carry it.

Sometimes late at night, after a day when it had been opened a lot, she would take it off and open it once more. She would pull things out one by one and remember when and why they were added. It held millions of small things, and a few huge things. There were also dark things, way deep down. She rarely took those out because she feared everyone would see them. There were things in there she didn't even remember; yet she carried their weight as well.

It was easy for her to be humble, as she only had to think about the dark bundle beneath her clothes. But some days she wondered if she was confusing depression with humility—or worse, if the price of humility was despondency. Knowing your darkness and carrying that knowledge must be the way it was. She could see no other way.

Maybe the problem was she was so attached to her backpack. Everything in it was a piece of her. She wanted to keep it just as much as she wanted freedom from it. It was part of her life; it carried the broken pieces of her heart. If she didn't keep it with her she'd never be able to put it all back together. It was getting so heavy, but she couldn't stop adding to it. She needed help so badly. She finally decided to ask The Father.

∾ ∾ ∾

Going to Him was hard. He was perfect, and she felt so tainted. She tried to wash before going to His house. But the more she tried, the more dirt she found, till it seemed as if she was dirtier than when she'd begun. She approached His house, feeling like death. He was there as usual. And she entered, feeling naked and ashamed. Clutching her backpack, she fell on her face at His feet. Her guilt washed over her, and she could not speak—only groan from deep inside.

She lay at His feet sobbing, until she realized He had gotten down onto the floor with her. He reached out and touched her. The Father was going to get her dirt on Him! Revulsion at her tainted body made her sick; she pulled back into a corner.

"Are you My child?" He asked. She wasn't sure how to answer. He took a step forward. "Are you My child?" She felt so confused. He took another step toward her. "Are you My child?" She knew the answer, although she didn't believe it.

"Yes," she said. She shook as He took the final step forward.

"Does that not make Me your Father?"

"Yes," she responded. "Yes, You're The Father."

"No, I am not just *The* Father, I am *your* Father." He reached out for her then. She pulled further back.

"I don't think I'm ready to give this up," she said, clutching her backpack.

"Tell Me what's in it."

She opened it and pulled out suffering, pain, confusion; lots and lots of sin; she pulled out sorrow and depression, and she pulled out guilt. Oh, so much guilt. It was full of guilt. She went to put it all away again, but He took her hands in His. He told her to feel His wrists. He took off His shoes and told her to put her hands on the scars in His feet. He talked to her about how He had already paid the price for her guilt, 2000 years before. Told her that she had been carrying it all this time not because she had to but because she wanted to. He had asked her for it over and over, and she had refused Him.

"You are My child. You became My child the first time we met, and from that moment on you were justified." He held her hands again, and she felt His scars as He spoke. "I have no condemnation for you, but you belong to Me—don't forget who you are. I am going to rename you. I'm going to call you Full-of-Grace so that you never forget what I have given you."

She looked down at the spilled contents of her backpack, but they were all gone. As she turned to go, she bent to pick up the empty sack she had always carried. "Leave it—it belongs to Me." She looked up at Him. "I paid for it," He said, smiling.

Therefore, no condemnation now exists
for those in Christ Jesus, because the Spirit's law of life
in Christ Jesus has set you free from the law of sin and of death.
—Romans 8:1-2

THE END

My 23-year-old daughter wrote "The Backpack Story" in the middle of a sleepless night. Her name, Anita, means "full of grace." Anita's story so clearly illustrates in allegorical form the core message of grace. Her story encapsulates the theme of this book: The Father comes to us in our wilderness, He calls us to Him, He removes our burdens, He reminds us we are His beloved children, and He gives us hope and a future purpose.

A Ring on His Finger

I was raised in a religious home and attended church regularly with my family, but I found it empty and meaningless. I determined to shuck religion as soon as I lived on my own. And that's what I did after moving to a city to attend the university. But just four months later, the God who pursues found me and brought me into His kingdom. My life was radically altered, and with Pauline zeal I wanted to tell everyone I knew.

I cooked up a plot to break the news to my parents, who, I knew, would not welcome the news that I had forsaken their religious tradition. The plan was this: My boyfriend and I, both new converts, were a singing duo. We offered to sing a song in his parents' evangelical church in our hometown. I invited my parents to the service but didn't tell them I would be speaking before we sang.

My parents were staunch, lifelong members of a mainline church in their small town. The only time they ever attended other churches was for weddings, funerals, or bake sales. They were discouraged from worshiping outside their denomination. So the fact that my parents even attended this service was already a huge stretch for them. They sat on the back row by the door. I can see them still in my mind's eye, stiff and wary in the last pew.

I gave my talk, bubbling over with enthusiasm about my new life in Christ. I don't remember much of what I said other than this accusation, which shattered my mother's heart and carelessly disregarded her dignity: "Before coming to Christ, I didn't even know what a Christian was," I proclaimed with a wide grin on my face. More than 30 years later, I hang my head in shame when I recall that scene.

At home, my mother's initial reaction was to retreat to her bedroom, where she cloistered herself and wept for two days. But before she went she told me with trembling lips that what I had done to her and my dad that day had hurt her worse than the death of another daughter a few years earlier in a tragic car accident. I was sorry for her pain but had no concept of its origin or depth.

Slowly, over time, God opened my eyes to the truth. I came to see that dreadful hour through their eyes. I had humiliated my parents in front of their neighbors, co-workers, and friends. By claiming that "I didn't know what a Christian was," I was declaring them to be pagans. Had they not raised me in a Christian church and tried to live as Christians all their life? Of course they had. In addition to that, while I had blithely testified to finding salvation, throwing it in their face like a weapon, they believed I had forsaken God and heaven by rejecting my original baptism.

Bluntly, they thought I was headed for hell. My mother's pain came more out of concern for my eternal destiny than for what I perceived to be embarrassment or humiliation at my public "crossing the religious floor."

∾∾∾

As I matured and had children of my own I slowly awakened to the horror and the truth of what I had done. I also realized that after that weekend, my mother never spoke of it again or treated me any differently than she always had. In other words, she forgave me and reinstated me in her heart and life. And she went one step further.

During the last few months of her life, as cancer claimed more and more of her strength and vitality, my siblings and I took turns staying with her and caring for her. Our father had passed away a few years earlier, leaving her alone in her mid-60s. During one of my last visits she asked me to help divide up her belongings between her remaining seven children. I itemized everything in the house, and we went through the list together.

When I thought the list was complete, she added two more things. "I want Paulette to have my wedding band," she said to me late one night. I heartily agreed, knowing that my oldest sister had walked through many trials with Mom. She deserved that special memento.

But what she said next, I will never forget. "And I want you to have my diamond ring."

I was speechless with shame and surprise. "I don't deserve it," I stammered, choking up.

"I want you to have it," she replied. The topic was closed.

Even though my mother and I had never again mentioned the

incident I described earlier, I had never forgotten it. And I was sure she hadn't either. I knew how badly I had wounded her—how I wished I could turn back the clock and rewrite the history of that dreadful hour!

Like the prodigal son, I was overwhelmed with the generosity of spirit of my injured parent: "The father told his slaves, 'Quick! Bring out the best robe and put it on him; put a ring on his finger and sandals on his feet'" (Luke 15:22). Like the prodigal son, I had squandered my religious inheritance and wandered far away. Instead of rejecting me or reducing me to a lower status, my mother demonstrated grace by putting a ring on my finger.

Thankfully, even though I had always found it hard to have any intimacy with my mother and she with me, I was able to tell her how I felt. When I tucked her into bed that night, I haltingly said, "Mom—you have taught me more about Christian love and forgiveness than anyone else in my life. Thank you." I smiled a shaky smile as tears pooled in my eyes. She responded with a small smile and a nod and looked away. It was a moment of healing for me and, I hope, for her too. I am so grateful that God gave me the opportunity to make amends before it was too late.

After Mom died, I was given her ring, a ring with four tiny diamonds in it. I wore it next to my wedding band. A few months later, when I noticed one of those diamonds had disappeared, I took the ring to a jeweler and had the three remaining stones imbedded in my wedding band. This little trinity of glitter is a constant reminder to me of God's grace as lived out in my mother's life.

What's So Amazing About Grace?

In Philip Yancey's book about grace, the central question is just what the title asks—what *is* so amazing about grace? The answer to that question is, grace is scandalous. It doesn't make sense. It shocks us. It might even make us mad. Grace isn't fair. It wasn't fair that my mother gave me, of all her children, that diamond ring. But she did it from a heart of grace. She wanted me to know, without a doubt, that she loved me. Perhaps she thought her other children did not need that extra reassurance. I'll never know until we are reunited in heaven.

Only God could think up something as reckless as grace. Humans cannot comprehend the depth of love it takes to come up with such a scandalous plan for salvation, let alone apply grace to sinful man. "Grace means there is nothing we can do to make God love us more…And grace means there is nothing we can do to make God love us less."[1]

I don't know about you, but I still don't get this. I talk about it, write about it, even claim to believe it, but can I live it?

> Put bluntly: the American church today accepts grace in theory but denies it in practice. We say we believe that the fundamental structure of reality is grace, not works—but our lives refute our faith. By and large, the gospel of grace is neither proclaimed, understood, nor lived. Too many Christians are living in the house of fear and not in the house of love,[2]

writes Brennan Manning in *The Ragamuffin Gospel.*

Older-Brother Thinking

Let's return to the story of the lost son for a moment to hear the rest of the story:

> His older son was in the field; as he came near the house, he heard music and dancing. So he summoned one of the servants and asked what these things meant. "Your brother is here," he told him, "and your father

has slaughtered the fattened calf because he has him back safe and sound."

Then he became angry and didn't want to go in. So his father came out and pleaded with him. But he replied to his father, "Look, I have been slaving many years for you, and I have never disobeyed your orders; yet you never gave me a young goat so I could celebrate with my friends" (Luke 15:25-29).

In a radio address I heard recently, Chuck Swindoll referred to his book *The Grace Awakening* and summarized some of its message by listing five "grace killers."[3] I grabbed a pencil and jotted them down:

1. shame and guilt
2. legalistic rules and regulations
3. pettiness and a judgmental attitude
4. small-mindedness and king-of-the-mountain mentality
5. ecclesiastical abuse

The middle three have "older brother" written all over them: "That brat broke the rules! You're supposed to wait until your father dies to get your inheritance, like I have." "Why should we throw a party for him? He deserves a good beating for wasting his inheritance so foolishly. If he thinks I'll share my inheritance with him, he's crazy!"

Sadly, the church today is full of older brothers. Grace is preached from our pulpits but rarely practiced in our pews, Swindoll says. We judge others. We form cliques. We exclude those who don't measure up in their performance, dress, or connections.

We get mad when we see God's hand of blessing on our undeserving spiritual siblings who are "doing" so much less than we are. Squeaky clean, never late for church, serving on several committees, we are living as though we are trying to save up a down payment on the mansions Jesus promised to prepare *for* us in the next life.

The older brother continues to berate the father for welcoming the prodigal home so enthusiastically. He's so ticked off he can't even refer to him as his own brother:

> "When this son of yours came, who has devoured your assets with prostitutes, you slaughtered the fattened calf for him."
>
> "Son," he said to him, "you are always with me, and everything I have is yours. But we had to celebrate and rejoice, because this brother of yours was dead and is alive again; he was lost and is found" (Luke 15:30-32).

જ જ જ

Did you get the message? We "had to celebrate and rejoice," the father says. That is what I am talking about, fellow wanderer. God pursues us and finds us in our wilderness. He makes us alive again. Then He can't help Himself—He rejoices! The fact that God rejoices over the return of "a wretch like me," to quote the words of the most famous hymn ever written about grace, is shocking. It's scandalous. It doesn't seem fair to all my spiritual siblings who never wandered or squandered. Why should heaven rejoice over my return? Or yours? I can't explain it or hope to understand it. But I'm grateful for it.

Amazing grace, how sweet the sound, that saved a wretch like me.
I once was lost but now am found, was blind but now I see.[4]

Part Three

Long Day's Journey:
Living with Mature Faith

CHAPTER ELEVEN

Sweat Equity

Just as the body without the spirit is dead,
so also faith without works is dead.
The apostle James

Even if you're on the right track,
you'll get run over if you just sit there.
Will Rogers

*W*hether Habitat for Humanity was first to introduce the concept of sweat equity, I doubt. But they were the ones that brought it to my attention. Sweat equity, as a concept and a practice, can help the wanderer move forward along the road to mature faith.

What is sweat equity? The person or family who has been chosen by Habitat for Humanity to receive a new home is required to work a significant number of hours on the job site. In most cases, prospective Habitat homeowners make a $500 down payment and contribute 300 to 500 hours of "sweat equity" on the construction of their home or someone else's home.[1] Prospective homeowners are exempt from needing a large down payment, something they do not have, and are asked to contribute something they do have—effort and commitment. We all sweat! (Or as our mothers told us, "Women glow. Men perspire. Horses sweat.") I use the word *sweat* to denote disciplined effort.

This is a close approximation of the deal God makes with us. God offers us the free gift of salvation; no strings attached. We can't earn it; we can't buy it. It requires an act of the will on our part. The commitment is that we choose to believe He is our Savior and Controller. We agree He is God and we are not. We give Him complete access to our heart and total control of our life.

Wilderness Insurance

Buying hail insurance doesn't change the weather patterns. Hail will come. That's why farmers buy insurance. With insurance, if you get hailed out, at least you haven't lost everything, because the insurance broker will pay you some compensation for the loss. In the same way, there is no foolproof "insurance" against returning to the wilderness. However, being destroyed by a wilderness experience is less likely if you "buy into" a lifestyle that will keep you moving forward on the road to mature faith:

- Practice the spiritual disciplines of prayer, study, worship, and fellowship.
- Be real at church, at home, and in the marketplace; peel away the masks as God reveals them to you.
- Allow God to unveil and use your uniqueness for His purposes.
- Let Jesus be your Friend. Assume He loves you.
- Risk trusting Him again.

The chapters in this book's final part will deal with these topics.

Spiritual Disciplines

The wanderer will not make much headway with Christ until he or she embraces the spiritual disciplines of prayer, Bible study, worship, and service. These are all things we once did but that probably fell by the wayside the further we drifted. For instance, most wanderers stop reading their Bibles because they no longer find direction or comfort there. It may take months of regular Bible-reading before the Word once again comes to life and becomes relevant in the life of a recovering wanderer. But read on, by faith, because it *will* get better. I am intentionally keeping the list of spiritual disciplines short and simple because the road to mature faith is daunting enough. Another reason is because God has called me to tell the truth, and these four things are what I have done thus far. I cannot, in good conscience, recommend to you anything I am not practicing.

Now, some people don't like the word *discipline*. It evokes unpleasant memories of being punished or having privileges revoked. Discipline, when practiced, is nothing more than routine. Discipline and disciple are from the same root word, *discere*— "disciple: a learner; discipline: learning."[2] To be Christ's disciple requires discipline. Mark Buchanan calls spiritual disciplines

> holy habits: the disciplines, the routines by which we stay alive and focused on Him. At first we choose them and carry them out; after a while they are part of who we are. And they carry us.[3]

With every discipline we eventually cross that invisible barrier from "grin and bear it" to "hey, I like this!" What does it in every case are two things: perseverance and guidance.

When I decided, in my mid-40s, to take up jogging after a long hiatus, it was not fun. It hurt. The runs were painful, lung-searing, leg-aching experiences. After my paltry five kilometers, I would stagger home red-faced and wringing wet. But I kept on because I believed it would get better. It took more than a year of running three times per week before I was able to convincingly say it didn't hurt anymore. During that time I saw many other runners who made it look easy. They sprinted past me with grins on their faces as I grimaced and shuffled along. I persevered, believing that one day I would enjoy it too. For two years I ran "on faith." Finally, after the second year, I got to the point where the run was enjoyable. I could do five kilometers without too much strain, and it gave me energy to meet the day's demands. (I began to look forward to the run for energy as well as the chemical boost it offered that lightened my mood. Then my knees went. Ah well, c'est la vie!)

And so it is with spiritual disciplines. We all know people who spend regular time in prayer and Bible study, in worship and in service, and the joy of the Lord is evident in all they do and say. They prove it can be done. They give hope to wanderers who want what they have—connectedness with the Father. I'm "running" with some of them now. Oh, not every day—but I have more "good runs" than bad ones, and I press on, full of hope that He who promises is faithful.

About Guidance

By guidance, I mean that whenever you try to learn something new, like a sport, it helps to get some tips from an expert, to take lessons. After three years of trying to mortally wound myself on alpine skis, I decided to take a few lessons. Voilà! In a few minutes I received some valuable tips that revolutionized my technique and turned my downhill experience (pun intended) in a positive direction.

Guidance can come from healthy relationships. What the Lord led me to do was to walk alongside women who were serious about growing in their faith. He gave me good friends. Through shared Bible studies and hours of honest dialogue, I was challenged, held accountable, loved, and encouraged to develop a mature faith.

Guidance can also come from good books. There are plenty of books available on mentoring and spiritual direction, as well as on every aspect of the inner life one could imagine. I have devoured dozens of books, and I feel like the authors are my new "running mates." A weakness I have that I caution you about is that I tend to read too much and think too little. I have forced myself to slow down, to reread, to take notes, and to dialogue with others about the things I am learning. Don't let lack of funds hinder you. Exchange books with your friends. Get a library card. Start a church library if you don't already have one. Ask for books for birthday gifts. Find a good used bookstore.

> Our goal in developing mature faith is to re-establish (or acquire for the first time) some habitual practices that keep us spiritually "fit."

About Perseverance

After suffering enough pain in my left knee to cause me to stop jogging for several months, along with other treatment, I decided to stop crossing my legs. My physiotherapist mentioned that as a "bad habit." It was a habit I must have developed decades ago; I have no memory of starting it. However, I discovered how ingrained it was when I decided to try to break it. I have been a "non-crosser" for about a year now—and every single day, several times a day, I still catch myself attempting to swing one leg over the other "out of habit." Sitting on an inflated exercise ball at my desk helps me remember because if I do try to cross, I roll off the ball onto the floor!

Breaking habits is hard work. The corollary is that habits, once formed, become routine. We don't even think about them. Good habits are as easy to form as bad ones. Holy habits of prayer, Bible study, worship, and service, once formed, can also be hard to break. And that is to our advantage. When something becomes habitual, we miss it when it's not there. Our goal in developing mature faith is to re-establish (or acquire for the first time) some habitual practices that keep us spiritually "fit." Habits are formed by repetition over time. Holy habits are no different. Keep at it.

Bible Study

Bible-study classes are available at home, church, Bible college, or seminary. For the last few years, I have enrolled in one study in the fall or one in the spring or both. In addition to an endless variety of printed materials, there are great Bible studies available on CD, cassette, video, and DVD. Online opportunities are abundant and very good also. I have done a few of these and have also started auditing master's-level classes at a Baptist seminary nearby. Learning historical context and biblical background has greatly enlivened my interest in and understanding of Scripture. My husband gets a kick out of my questions. I called him on his cell phone at work this morning to ask, "Who are the Nicolaitans, and why did Jesus hate them?" (see Revelation 2).

Do not discount the guidance available to you through the wisdom and knowledge of others. My husband is my best resource. He never forgets anything he's ever read. Not only does he help our children with high-school physics problems some 30 years after his last physics class, he helps me with all sorts of biblical and theological information. Your pastor and perhaps some deacons and Bible-study teachers are great founts of wisdom available to you for the price of a shared cup of coffee or a phone call. (I caution you—stick with your own gender).

Journaling

Bill Hybels refers to journaling as an opportunity to replay the videotape of our day and do a "postgame analysis."[4] He introduced this discipline into his life years ago to aid him in his quest for genuine faith. As he traveled extensively and spoke, he met many other Christians who led and served. Journaling was something many of them practiced as a vital spiritual discipline.

Journaling has been something I have done off and on for most of my adult life. The deeper I wandered into the wilderness, the less I journaled. Then a friend and mentor named Willoughby sent me a beautifully bound book with lined pages as a Christmas gift. The journal had a deep purple cover, a gold spine, and a picture on the front of a luxuriant vine heavy with plump grapes. What better illustration of the life I so longed for? "Jesus says, 'I am the vine; you are the branches. The one who remains in me and I in him produces much fruit, because you can do nothing without me'" (John 15:5).

Along with the journal was a note challenging me to read the Word slowly, verse by verse, and record anything and everything the Lord brought to mind. And so I began in the wee hours of January first of a new year. "With a mixture of eager anticipation and fearful doubt, I begin this journey into journaling," I wrote. I went on for more than two pages talking about what I was finding in Scripture. Since I had found such renewal and hope in

Psalm 51, instead of starting with the Gospels as I had planned, I
went back to that psalm and reread it for the thousandth time. I
realize now that some of the things I jotted down that night form
the skeleton of this book. The last words I recorded were a prayer:
"God, give me discipline!"

One year and two days later, again after midnight, I wrote in
the last page of that purple journal. My opening words were, "Less
than 24 hours from now and it'll all be over!" What I meant by
that was, our firstborn was getting married the next day. I went on
to talk about the events of the day behind me, the fun of the
rehearsal dinner, the ups and downs of last-minute surprises, the
laughter and the tears. I ended that entry with this simple but
heartfelt prayer: "Thank You, Father, for Your grace and kindness
to me and to my family. Help me to be a good model for my children and others. I pray that my children would love You and know
You even more fully than I do. Amen." Throughout that year of
journaling and ever since, God has been helping me to live
authentically, not just for my benefit, but that others would see
Jesus in me. Have I ever failed? You bet I have. Have I ever quit?
Not yet.

My Postgame Analysis

Journaling my impressions as I read the Word has also been an
important element of my journey toward mature faith. After
experiencing months, sometimes years, of what I thought was
total silence from God, it is so encouraging to look back over my
journals and see the many times and many ways God really *had*
spoken to me. I am always surprised as I sift back through the
sporadic entries I made during my decade of dryness to see many
instances recorded of things He said to me through His Word or
through worship or the words of a godly friend. If I did not have

that record, how easily I might forget that God was actively pursuing me! He was near whether I sensed Him or not. There were many little oases in the desert I have forgotten but, thanks to the paper trail, the evidence of God's relentless pursuit is clear. What I thought was a decade of abandonment actually contained many little encounters between God and me that the enemy worked hard at making me forget.

Prayer

Praying silently is a surefire method to get me thinking all kinds of things—from planning menus, to wondering if my children will find suitable mates, to snoring and drooling. What begins as sincere prayer is easily sidetracked by daily concerns. Jotting down what I am praying not only disciplines the prayer, it is a good method to check up on myself.

Leaving a written record makes it easier to go back and see if your prayer life is balanced or narrowly focused. *Am I praying for people outside my family or just us? Am I praying for the physically sick but neglecting the spiritually sick? Am I just asking God for "stuff" or seeking to know Him? Am I worshiping God as I pray? Am I thanking God? Am I praising God?* As I read back over my prayers I realize how imbalanced I have been—lots of requests, too little worship and praise. Had I not been journaling, I would have no way of analyzing the content of my prayer life.

Journaling prayers also provides opportunities to record answers. Here and there in my journals are places I have gone back and written in His wonderful answers to prayers in the margins. Nothing makes me feel more connected to the Vine than knowing that His life is flowing through me, through intercessory prayer, to make a difference in the world. Sometimes the answers aren't the ones we expect. God may not send you the job, the spouse, the career you have prayed for—but He will send you what He purposes for your life. This too can be recorded as answered prayer. Because He's God and we're not, we should never assume we know the answers He will send. Instead we must pay attention to everything that happens in our lives and look for His creative involvement.

Worship

Worship happens both inside and outside the church. For the wanderer, worship becomes stale. The further we drift, the less we want to worship. We grow frustrated by the very notion that God wants to be worshiped. This God who does not seem to hear our cries or answer our prayers wants us to worship Him? How arrogant is that? Everything for Him, and nothing for me? Harrumph! And so we withdraw even further. But worship is such a simple thing. Returning from the wilderness has taught me that worship gives God pleasure because worship is simply being obedient.

As a parent, I feel pleasure when my children obey me. When they were little, obedience saved their lives. I insisted we hold hands while crossing streets and parking lots, and on many occasions that kept them from being struck and killed by inattentive drivers. I made sure they had regular bedtimes and healthy meals, and when my children went to bed on time and ate their vegetables, I was pleased. Obviously, the pleasure did not come from my need to be adored, it came from the reality that the rules I made were for their benefit, not mine. Rest, nutrition, traffic safety, curfews—all of these came out of my desire to see my kids experience the best life has to offer.

God wants that for us. Our vision is temporal, but He sees life as a continuum. It does not end here. Earth is only the beginning. The temporary trials we experience here prepare us for something far greater in *His* time. The sweat equity benefit of worship learned now will continue with us when we see Him face-to-face.

Every Act of Service Is an Act of Worship

Worship is doing what we can with what we have. As Rick Warren notes, "There are no unspiritual abilities, just misused ones."[5] When I was a college student I once had a summer job working in a peat-moss factory just outside my hometown. I was one of only two women who worked there. The job was hot and extremely dirty and, for a woman, brutally exhausting. We had to lift and carry large bales that could weigh more than a hundred pounds if the moss was wet. The owner of the factory was a family friend who knew how desperate I was for a job that year and he gave me a chance. I understood that for the sake of morale he wanted to keep our relationship on a business level and not show me any favoritism. He treated me like he did all the other factory workers.

One day he took me off the assembly line and assigned me a special job. Beneath a large conveyor belt that carried freshly harvested moss into the factory for cleaning, a pile would accumulate as it fell or blew off the belt. It gathered in a stub-walled cubbyhole under the lower end of the sloping conveyor. This room had about four feet of moss in it the day my boss asked me to shovel it out and wheelbarrow the contents to the area for processing.

I was a new believer at the time, but I had been well taught: Every act of service was an act of worship. And so I whistled and sang praise tunes and shoveled for several hours, stopping only for my regular breaks. Unbeknownst to me, my boss came by in the afternoon when I was about three-quarters finished and watched me for some time from the shadows. He surprised me when he appeared out of nowhere and, smiling, commented on how impressed he was by the way I steadily worked without supervision. What I knew in my heart but lacked the courage to say was that Someone *was* watching, and I wanted to please Him.

I found out a few years later that my silent witness did not go unnoticed. My former boss, who lost his life to cancer while still young, spoke to his family about that very incident after he received a letter from me. When I heard that he was terminally ill, I had written to him explaining my faith and outlining the way to become a child of God. He accepted my testimony partly because I had earned his respect on the factory floor many years earlier. God had given me the ability to shovel (dry moss is feather-light!), and that was an act of worship. "Based on the gift they have received, everyone should use it to serve others, as good managers of the varied grace of God" (1 Peter 4:10).

Worship Flows from a Grateful Heart

Worship, in its simplest form, is surrendering to God and agreeing to do what we can do. As we help and serve, worship, learn from the Word, and pray we grow and develop "until we all reach unity in the faith and in the knowledge of God's Son, growing into a mature man with a stature measured by Christ's fullness" (Ephesians 4:13). The recovering wanderer never forgets the desolation and spiritual isolation of the season of dry faith. That alone might be incentive enough to spur us to applying sweat equity to our spiritual life. But the greatest motivation comes from within. From a grateful heart. I rarely get out of church with dry eyes these days. I am often approached by well-meaning believers who have seen me weeping and have prayed that I be delivered from whatever is afflicting me. "Oh, no!" I have to tell them. "Don't ask God to stop *afflicting* me with gratitude!" Tears of gratitude that He did not forget me in my painful estate: As with Hannah, Sarah, Elizabeth, God looked upon my spiritual barrenness and brought forth new life. I weep with gratitude almost every time I hear the Word preached or sing His praises.

Worship Comes from a Healthy Heart

"What are you doing these days to care for your heart?"[6] John Eldredge once asked a small group of friends, as he writes in his book *Waking the Dead*. No one had an answer. Because "our heart matters to God," Eldredge says, we need to make sure to keep it healthy and fit as well. How do we build heart health? By doing what we love to do. If I gave you a ten-day holiday, all expenses paid, where would you go? What would you do? Would you be scouring the beach for shells at the seaside? Or screaming your head off riding the Drop of Doom at a theme park? Or curled up with a good book on the verandah of a cabin in the mountains? Or strolling along the wide boulevards of Paris, France? Or window-shopping at the Mall of America? Or puttering in your flower garden? Or playing a computer game? Or napping in a pool of sunlight like a well-fed cat? What refreshes you? What do you do when you need to rest? Whatever it is, that is how you care for your heart. Schedule some time for "heart health."

∾ ∾ ∾

Have you ever sat in a sauna or a steam bath? Talk about a great way to relax—you allow your own sweat to cleanse your pores and wash your cares away. It cleanses me, relaxes me, renews me, and warms me to the core. Sweat is a good thing. It is how our overheated bodies cool down. People who can't sweat have to find artificial ways to reduce their body temperature. As we sweat, our body relaxes and is "normalized." In the same way, the sweat of spiritual disciplines normalizes my life, helping to make me more balanced and healthy. So go ahead, "sweat it out"—develop some holy habits. As you jog along the road to mature faith, find some running mates who will encourage you, challenge you, and keep you accountable.

CHAPTER TWELVE

Unmasking

I know your works; you have a reputation
for being alive, but you are dead.
Jesus' words in the letter to the church in Sardis

There is no Concorde that flies us from immaturity to
maturity in a few hours. There is only a narrow, bumpy road
where a few people walk together as they journey to God.
Larry Crabb

Susan is one of my walking partners. Our walks are a chance to "do coffee" and get exercise at the same time. Susan is bright, well-educated, fun-loving, and "connected" to God. When I first met her I was deep in the wilderness and, although I was drawn to her wit and intellect, I was intimidated by her spirituality. She once suggested we pray together. Fear gripped my heart when she said that. Prayer was tough to fake, even though I had been a drama star in high school! I knew that if we met to pray, she would see the truth about my superficial relationship with God. I wasn't ready to take off the mask with her. I had played peek-a-boo with my mask with one or two other trusted friends, but I still did not know her well enough to take that risk. I managed to sidestep that invitation and Susan, who must have seen through my exterior game, refused to judge me or give up on me.

In my wilderness journey, when I began getting calls out of the blue to speak at women's events, I felt so unworthy, so spiritually unprepared, so scared. Like Moses, I kept arguing with God and asking Him to "send Aaron." But in the end, I always obeyed and went. Every time I had to prepare for a talk, though, I was a nervous wreck. I despaired that the wrong person had been asked to speak and that Susan or someone "spiritual" like her should go in my place. Susan tried to encourage me by validating my main area of giftedness—the ability to make audiences laugh by telling stories. Being comedic was not on any scale of spiritual gifts I had ever seen! Susan explained to me that everyone is unique, that my gift of humor was no less God-given than her ability as a professor to inform and inspire.

Get Real

One day Susan called and asked if I had time to squeeze in a walk. We hadn't walked for weeks because life had dished up a few extra helpings on both our plates. I missed our visits and although I greatly desired to go, I told her I was too busy.

"What are you busy with?" she asked.

"I have to get ready for a talk I'm giving tomorrow night."

"What do you still have to do?" Susan asked, like a good friend would. "Maybe I can help."

I gave her the whole scoop in one breathless sentence. "I have to highlight my hair, darken my eyebrows, file my heels, tweeze my chin, bleach my teeth, borrow that green-silk pantsuit from Kathy, glue on fake fingernails and paint them red—and I still haven't finished preparing my talk."

When I paused to take a breath, she asked, "What's your topic?"

"Being real—you know, being yourself," I responded. Her hoot of laughter clued me in to the absurdity of what I had said, and I realized I really did need to get out for a walk! Can we risk being real? Do we dare take off our mask? By breaking the conspiracy of silence about my wilderness, I took off a mask I had worn for years. Over time, I revealed that I did not have unshakable faith, but rather was plagued with doubt and struggling with unbelief. I revealed I was afraid of God and had spent years protecting myself from what I thought was His will.

Unmasking is not an event, it's a lifestyle. No sooner do I remove one mask than God reveals to me another. We wear more layers of paint than a century-old farmhouse. The ditches and gutters alongside the road to mature faith are littered with discarded masks.

Why Do We Wear Masks?

There are usually reasons why people wear masks. It only takes one or two times of being betrayed, humiliated, embarrassed, mocked, or disdained before people learn to wear a smiley face and hold others at a safe distance. This is as true—maybe more so—in the church as in the marketplace. The church is sometimes guilty of promoting a holier-than-real image of the Christian life. And I have been guilty also.

The first evangelical church I joined was unusual. I did not know this for years until I attended other churches and saw the contrast. One thing that made us different was that most of the members were under 25 years old, were university students, and were new Christians from nonevangelical families. We were all too young and naive to know that we needed to hide our sins. It was common knowledge among the group that this girl had a criminal record, that girl had given up a baby for adoption, the other girl had had an abortion, that guy had been a drug user, the other guy had a drinking problem, still another had been kicked out by his parents who were fed up with his poor choices, while another had flunked out of college because he'd stopped attending classes. We were sinners and we all knew it. Each of us had come to Christ for cleansing, for healing, for forgiveness, for grace. The church gave us the teaching we were so hungry for, it connected us with other followers who were on the same road, and it gave us a place to find unconditional love and acceptance.

Later, when my husband and I moved to California with our toddlers we joined a church in San Francisco. They had a wonderful team of pastors and many young families. With eager anticipation we dropped off our little girls in the nursery and attended our first adult Sunday-school class.

Learning to Hide

After welcoming new guests the teacher asked for prayer requests. That particular morning I was feeling pretty low. All week things had been difficult as I had tried to unpack and make our tiny apartment feel homey. Our two preschool daughters had "helped" by making wall murals with crayons, flushing trash down the toilet, building sandcastles in the tub with smuggled sand from outdoors...you get the picture. The real problem was that I was more concerned with cleaning the already clean apartment to get it "up" to my standards than I was about my children's need for my attention. I thought the girls were in the way. I spent the whole week shooing, scrubbing, and fussing at them. I had yelled at them more than once in anger and frustration as I discovered their latest creative attempt to make our home "pwetty."

When the teacher asked for prayer requests, I was the first one to speak up. Before two words were out of my mouth, tears were running down my face. "I need prayer," I blubbered. "I yell at my kids and I need to stop. I want to be a better mother." My confession was met with stunned silence as all eyes in the room were everywhere but on me. People looked up, some looked down, some leafed through their Bibles, some looked away. After a minute that felt like an hour, the teacher cleared his throat nervously and asked if anyone else had a request. The others in the room asked for prayer for salvation for lost friends and co-workers, healing for the sick, traveling mercies for those who were away, and spiritual blessing for missionaries. No one else asked for personal prayer to help with a sin problem. I did not speak again for the remainder of the hour.

After being dismissed we filed through narrow hallways toward the sanctuary. A classmate got my attention and pulled me aside. "Thank you for sharing so honestly," she began. "I know we all sin and need prayer, but for some reason—and I'm not sure why—we never talk about it in church. I'm glad you had the guts to do it." Her words soothed my humiliation, but the lesson had been learned. Not wanting to be different, I kept quiet about my sins—and the next time prayer was requested, I mentioned some third-party concerns that fit the criteria. I fit in. Today, more than two decades later, I am still peeling off the layers of the masks I have worn ever since I learned not to tell the truth in church about my sinful life at home.

❧ ❧ ❧

I believe the single, most compelling reason we wear masks is because of our need for approval. This is normal. People who do not care what others think are usually antisocial or, in extreme cases, amoral. I wear a mask because I believe that if others knew the real me, they would reject me. Jesus said that He came for the sick and the sinful, not the healthy. It sure seems like we have forgotten that in today's church. When we get ready for church, we do everything we can to disguise our sin and cover up our weaknesses. Even the simple act of walking forward in church to respond to an altar call is unthinkable for some of us. Walking the aisle would let others know we have problems that need pastoral prayer. Way too revealing!

Getting the Mask Off

Andrew and Mattie met through mutual friends at church and fell in love. Marriage was a serious topic of conversation right from the beginning. Their families were delighted and affirmed them. But somewhere along the way the couple ran into trouble. Even though they were regular in church and seemed to be growing in their faith, they did not take the necessary precautions to protect themselves from getting too physical. One night, they went too far. After many tears of remorse, they promised God and each other it would never happen again. But it did.

Not long after they announced their engagement, they discovered Mattie was pregnant. Initially they told no one and pondered their choices. They briefly considered abortion, thinking their secret would be too humiliating for their "respectable" parents to bear. Fortunately, this temptation quickly passed, and they realized they must tell their families and go ahead with the wedding as planned. Mattie and Andrew stopped attending Sunday services. They felt unworthy and humiliated.

Their pastor met with them privately one morning. They told him everything. Together, Andrew and Mattie decided to go to the church, admit their sin, and ask for forgiveness.

At the close of a service soon after, instead of saying a benediction, the pastor began to talk about the unconditional love of God and the role of the church in extending God's grace to others. He choked up as he referred to the cost Christ had paid for our forgiveness. "We, as a church, need to gather around and forgive two of our own children who have sinned but have truly repented before God." He beckoned Andrew and Mattie to join him at the front. With tears streaming down their faces, they walked forward, stood on either side of the pastor, and linked arms with him. I am moved even now, these many years later, as I recall that moment.

The assembled congregation was invited to extend Christ's love to this couple. Instantly, people left their seats and formed a long line down the center aisle. Mattie's grandfather, a retired missionary, was first, and he encircled them in a great bear hug. Tears flowed freely as people stepped forward. Some whispered their own secrets to the couple, admitting they had made the same mistake or one similar but had never shared it publicly and had carried the burden for decades.

Although no one has tallied the results of that incredible day, I will never forget it. Love was expressed, forgiveness was freely given, courage was rewarded, grace was manifested—God was there in such a real way. Church, the way God intended, happened! And all because one young couple chose to tell the truth, to be real, to take off the mask and allow others to share their experience.

How Do We Take It Off?

James reflects the heart of Jesus when he writes, "Confess your sins to one another and pray for one another, so that you may be healed" (James 5:16). There is healing in confession. Unacknowledged sin is the enemy's greatest advantage. Secrets are the fuel of blackmail. Without the secret, there can be no blackmail. Satan holds us hostage as long as we keep secrets and refuse to confess our sin. We remove our masks by confessing, first to God and then to others as He directs.

Something unkind I had done troubled me for years. Over a ten-year span, this recurring memory almost became an obsession. By the end of that decade, I thought of it many times a day—and each time the shame was so great and the memory so vivid, I would wince. At wits' end, one day I raised my hands and eyes to heaven and audibly confessed. Immediately my mind was flooded with the words, *I forgive you, I forgive you, I forgive you.* Tears welled up as I experienced a powerful sense of the Father's loving presence.

Not much later, the troubling emotions returned. I knew I had to take the second step of obedience—that of swallowing my pride and seeking forgiveness from the person I had wounded. My hands shook as I prepared to type an e-mail, so great was my humiliation. Amazingly, the miracle of cleansing happened as soon as I began to type. I felt completely clean before God once the letter was written and sent. "If we confess our sins, he is faithful and just and will forgive us our sins and purify us from all unrighteousness" (1 John 1:9 NIV). This verse says nothing about whether or not your confession brings the desired forgiveness from the one you have wronged. That is nice but not necessary. The act of confession in itself brings healing. An added bonus was that my "victim" immediately replied and told me he had no memory of the event and that I was unconditionally forgiven. What freedom!

Why in the world did I wait ten years? Fear of rejection probably had something to do with it. Don't be afraid,

> for we do not have a high priest who is unable to sympathize with our weaknesses, but we have one who has been tempted in every way, just as we are—yet without sin. Let us then approach the throne of grace with confidence, so that we may receive mercy and find grace to help us in our time of need (Hebrews 4:15-16).

Confess any and every sin He reveals to you. Allow the cleansing power of confession to revitalize your faith.

It's important, though, to choose your audience carefully. As I said earlier, we remove our masks by confessing to God and to others as He directs. Not every confession needs to be made in front of an entire congregation. Nor should it be. Most churches have small groups that meet on Sunday mornings or midweek for Bible studies. This is also your "church." These smaller groups are a good place for us to be real and transparent.

We Don't Graduate

I doubt there are many homes without some small pencil marks on a wall or door frame that indicate the children's growth patterns. I have some marks on the kitchen wall measuring my son's last few spurts. I just measured JP the other day, and he was in exactly the same spot he was several months ago. I assume he's now as tall as he's going to get. He is only 16 years old and still has a ways to go before reaching "maturity." His physical growth skyward is finished, but aspects of his character will continue to develop for decades.

We never stop growing. But there is this idea in Christendom that believers graduate. We've learned all there is to know. We're done. We're perfect. We're sinless. Well, we learn all right! We learn which sins are acceptable and which are not, and we pay lip service to the right behavior and attitudes. It's okay to eat too much or take a handful of pills for a headache caused by fatigue from overwork. Why not wash it down with some cola so you can go another mile before collapsing? It's okay to sleep too little and work too hard—those are "sins" we blink at. More than that, we see them as virtues. But heaven help us if we fantasize about the organist or sneak into a pub or lie on our tax returns or feel like slugging the guy who cuts us off in traffic. Neither you nor I would dare admit such behavior or ask for prayer for it at the Wednesday-night prayer service.

> You will discover that people still love you and accept you and even approve of you. Why? Because we are all the same. None of us is perfect. Those who are spiritually mature are the first to admit this.

If we want to stay out of the wilderness we must peel away our masks and quit faking our spirituality. Find or form a small group of people you can trust from your community of faith and be honest with them. Risk saying, "I yell at my kids and I want to stop." Maybe another mom will come alongside you, sharing her own experience with the same problem. Take a chance on admitting, "I am out of control in my eating and I need help." A Christian brother with the same weakness now knows how to pray and how to help you. Confess your struggles with road rage, or lust, or depression, or impulse buying, or unbelief, and allow others a peek behind the mask. Give them the chance to affirm you and encourage you, to pray for you and walk shoulder-to-shoulder with you toward wellness.

And believe it or not, you will discover that people still love you and accept you and even approve of you. Why? Because we are all the same. None of us is perfect. Those who are spiritually mature are the first to admit this.

An Authenticity Gap

God sent me a good friend during the four years we lived in a North Saskatchewan village as a newlywed couple. Marie-Louise, born and raised in the Netherlands, had married a Canadian market-gardener named Jim, whom she'd met when she made her first trip to Canada in the early 1970s. Marie-Louise and Jim lived directly across the lake from us. Their house sat atop a six-acre garden that sloped all the way down to the lake. We met through our husbands' shared interest in "all things green" and quickly bonded. Marie-Louise and I had much in common: We both had tiny children, families that lived far away, careers we had abandoned in favor of full-time motherhood, the love of good books, back-to-the-land lifestyles, and a deep commitment to God.

Because Marie-Louise was a member of the denomination I had eschewed in favor of an evangelical church, I assumed that even though she spoke freely about God, she must not be a born-again believer. I thought it was my job to introduce her to a personal relationship with Christ. So I "witnessed" to Marie-Louise every chance I got. I was "intentional" as I dove in with both barrels blazing. I seldom let an opportunity pass without throwing in some kind of spiritual sales pitch.

We shared many pots of tea steeped on the wood-burning stove in the kitchen of her rustic cottage. Marie-Louise good-naturedly defended her church and belief system, and even after my husband and I moved to a nearby city, our friendship continued long-distance. Because I was not convinced that Marie-Louise knew Jesus like I did, I felt like I hadn't done my job.

Let me say that there was nothing about Marie-Louise's lifestyle that caused me to doubt her salvation; it was that I couldn't get her to use the same terminology we used in the evangelical church. I wanted to hear her say she had "accepted Jesus." I wanted to know she had "asked Jesus to come into her heart." She steadfastly refused to adopt my lingo—and so I thought I had failed. I thought I must not have been a good witness.

∽∽∽

Several months after we moved, Marie-Louise was in the city, and she dropped by for a visit. *Aha!* I thought. *This may be my last chance to witness to her before we leave the country.* We both knew that once summer came, my family was moving to California. When she arrived, I was genuinely happy to see her, and we talked furiously, catching up on all the news since we had last seen each other. Unable to relax, I constantly tried to steer the conversation toward spiritual things to create an opening for a clear gospel presentation.

The harder I worked, the more puzzled Marie-Louise appeared. Finally, she took a deep breath and began to speak more slowly and carefully. "I have so enjoyed our friendship," she began.

"Me too!" I interrupted, planning to use that as a lead-in to a discussion of my friend Jesus. But she cut me off.

"No, please don't interrupt," she continued. I clamped my lips together, a bit surprised by the intensity of her expression. "I felt so delighted and surprised to find a friend like you in this remote place," she went on, referring to her life on the farm where we had been neighbors. "I was also glad to find someone who was as interested in spiritual things as I am. I have enjoyed our discussions"—she paused—"for the most part." She paused again, weighing her words carefully so as to be accurate but not offensive. I waited. "But lately I have the impression you don't think my church is as good as yours. That you think I should change something. I can't shake the feeling that you're trying to sell me something…and I don't like it. Why can't we just be friends?"

I was stunned. She had me. I was no different from a pushy peddler hawking his wares from town to town. But I couldn't admit it yet, so I rashly denied her astute assessment, reassuring her we were good friends and she had misinterpreted my motives. I bustled around preparing another pot of tea, hoping to hide my face that was red with embarrassment.

Hours later, after our good-byes were said and hugs exchanged, after my babies were sleeping and I was soaking in a hot bath, I pondered her words. They stung. I still did not want to admit she'd been right. I was confused and hurt as I called out to God: *I thought I was supposed to witness to people!* It would be many years before I could recall that experience without shame. Over the next several years I struggled with the question, What is a good witness?

Being an Unmasked Witness

In Paul's second letter to the church in Corinth, he talks about the open door for service and speaking out that he encountered: "When I arrived in Troas to proclaim the Message of the Messiah, I found the place wide open: God had opened the door; all I had to do was walk through it" (2 Corinthians 2:12 MSG). He goes on to describe how believers give off a "sweet scent rising to God" as they go about their daily lives. This aroma of Christ either draws seekers to Him or drives cynics away. Paul goes on to distinguish between a peddler of the gospel and one who genuinely attempts to share the gift with others:

> We are not, as so many, peddling the word of God; but as of sincerity, but as from God, we speak in the sight of God in Christ (verse 17 NKJV).

In Eugene Peterson's rendering:

> At least we don't take God's Word, water it down, and then take it to the streets to sell it cheap. We stand in Christ's presence when we speak; God looks us in the face. We get what we say straight from God and say it as honestly as we can (verse 17 MSG).

Kevin Cavanaugh (no relation), a pastor in British Columbia, illustrated one of his points in a workshop I attended by drawing two circles on a whiteboard with a space between them. In one of the circles he wrote "GOD" and in the other he wrote "MAN." Then he drew a little stick figure in the middle and wrote "YOU." "You see this gap between God and man?" he asked. "This is the authenticity gap, and you stand in it." His point was that when the world looks for God, they look to us and through us—the believers. If we are authentic, if we are transparent, we offer a clear window through which they can see God. If we are hiding behind a perfectionist mask, we misrepresent authentic Christianity; we misrepresent Christ.

Tell Both Sides of the Truth

When I was "marketing Jesus" I had a tendency to withhold some of the truth. I wasn't exactly lying, I told myself, I was just deciding whether or not the person I was making my sales pitch to was ready to hear the whole truth. If you were selling your car, would you purposely omit telling the prospective buyer about the warped gasket? The radiator leak? The collision repair hidden under a paint job? I hope not. Why then do we tell seekers all the best selling features of the Christian life and not include the reality that the road ahead will have some rough sections? An unmasked Christian must tell both sides of the truth.

Read Jesus' conversation with the rich young ruler in Matthew 19. Jesus never pulled any punches. When the man asked Him what "good thing" he needed "to do to get eternal life," Jesus focused in on the man's choice of words: "Why do you question me about what's good? God is the One who is good. If you want to enter the life of God just do what he tells you" (verses 16-17 MSG). Jesus is trying to let the man know that it is not a question of works, of *doing* something to earn eternal life—it is a matter of the heart, of surrendering to the Father. Still unclear, the rich man probes further: "What in particular?" (verse 18 MSG). He is still trying to find out what he must *do*. Jesus lists several of the Ten Commandments. The young man replies that he has kept all of Moses' laws. So then Jesus hits him with the whole enchilada: "Go sell your possessions; give everything to the poor. All your wealth will then be in heaven. Then come follow me" (verse 21 MSG). At this, the rich man walks away, empty-hearted.

Jesus did not spin out just enough of the truth to hook the guy, planning to break the rest of the story to him on a "need to know" basis. He told the young man the whole truth: If you want a relationship with God that results in eternal life, you must give up everything you have, even your very life, and follow. At that point, the rich man made a choice based on the complete evidence—he chose to keep his earthly wealth and forfeit heavenly wealth. He said no.

Keep Your Story Straight

As part of my unmasking, I decided to try to use the same vocabulary and subject matter with all my friends. I started with my walking partners—some of whom were Christian, some not. Regardless of which person I was out with, I tried to tell the same stories in the same way. If God was to be praised, I praised Him in front of each of them. If I was upset or saddened by something that happened in my family or church, I confided in all of them. If I was praying about a concern, I told them all.

This genuineness has not hindered my relationships with nonbelievers. If anything, it has improved them. My willingness to be real, to expose my warts, leads to opportunities to freely discuss spiritual things. Does that mean some people will reject the message and choose to not believe? Yes—as we saw, even Jesus experienced that. That example alone should convince us to "keep our story straight."

If an unbeliever thinks Christians don't have troubles, she is in for one huge surprise when she becomes a believer. If we don't tell the whole truth, and someone does place her trust in Christ on that basis, what do you think will happen to her when she's hit with her first crisis of faith? She'll think she's the only one who's ever had such a crisis. She'll think she's a bad Christian. She'll feel abandoned, and alone, and ashamed. She'll wonder why everyone else seems to have such confidence and security in their Christian walk and she battles doubt. She'll question whether God is who she thinks He is, whether her faith is misplaced, whether the Bible is true. And she may even give up and walk away from her faith because no one told her it would be so hard.

∽∽∽

Unmasking is simply a call for authenticity. Most of us went through a time in our teens and early adulthood of trying to "find ourselves." Young people are often blown this way and that depending on which wind is strongest. But most of us eventually figure out what we value and what we want to do with our life. If you become a believer later in life, you get to go through this soul-search twice! The wilderness caused me to rethink and find my spiritual self all over again. The "me" I found (am still finding) wants to be real, wants to be transparent, wants to be confessional. If I can be true to God and myself, regardless of earthly opinion, I am well on my way to a mature faith.

CHAPTER THIRTEEN

There's Only One You

She has done a noble thing for me...
She has done what she could.
Jesus

What we really are matters more than
what other people think of us.
Jawaharlal Nehru

*D*uring the four years we lived in Quebec, I began to flounder and lose my way. Prior to moving to this French-speaking province, I had been a pastor's wife with clearly defined roles. The move to Quebec was also a job change for my husband, so I was no longer in the position I had grown accustomed to and comfortable with. In Quebec my bilingual husband, Gerry, was quickly at home and able to communicate in French as his new job required. But I did not speak the language, and for the first time, I was not able to be involved in my husband's work. I didn't know what to do. The arrival of our third child coincided with this move, as did the discovery that my mother had terminal cancer. These factors alone were enough to throw me off balance—and I called out to God for guidance, asking Him what my "job" was. I heard no clear answer.

I voiced my feelings of uncertainty with my husband's colleague one day. "I don't know what I'm supposed to do," I said.

"What would you like to do?" he asked.

I had seldom been asked that question, so it caught me off guard. Up until then, I had been part of small churches where most of the members simply did what needed doing. The needs were endless, and the workers were few. We didn't stop to figure out if we were working from our area of strength or giftedness, we just dove in and got the job done. Whether it was working with children, teaching Vacation Bible School, painting the fence, scrubbing toilets, or gathering windblown garbage from the parking lot, my method of service for the Lord had always involved responding to obvious needs.

Intrigued by his question, I mustered up my courage and tentatively offered my honest answer. "I think I'd like to speak to women's groups," was my nervous, halting reply.

There was a lull as he considered this. He looked off into the distance, pondering. I waited, confidence waning. About the time I was tempted to check his pulse, he finally offered, "Wouldn't you have to have something to say?"

∽∽∽

Ouch! In my naiveté I thought I had plenty to say, but God knew better. He saw the big picture. I still had a desert to cross. Only later would I learn that my years in the wilderness would be instrumental in giving me "something to say." My wilderness would be the school for the soul where I came to know the real God from a position of brokenness; where I developed empathy, compassion, and understanding for fellow wanderers; and where I learned to trust Him enough to face my fear and surrender to

His call. Amid the sandstorm of doubt, He taught—is teaching—me to be authentic, to tell the truth, and to rely on Him to do His kingdom work through me and in me as I respond in obedience to His "drawing in" and "sending out."

Our Simple Gift

Every believer is called by God to make a difference for Christ in the world. For the sake of clarity, I will call this "difference" your *ministry*. Some people don't like that word. It scares them. They have visions of giving up everything they have worked hard for, saying good-bye to those they love, and sailing off to faraway jungles to spread the gospel using hand signals.

But I define ministry as "doing what I can do for Jesus." That's it. Especially for women, there are times in our life where we can do much and times when it seems like we are doing little for Him in the public arena. There have been short seasons in my life where it was all I could do to keep my babies in clean diapers, put nutritious food on the table, keep my husband's shirts ironed, and take my regular rotation in the nursery at church. I didn't teach, sing, play an instrument, or organize even the simplest event. My ministry at that time involved primarily caring for my family and responding to simple needs in the community of faith as they arose—things like bringing a meal to a bereaved family, caring for the toddler of a sick mom, or bringing snacks to a midweek Bible study.

There have been other seasons in which I was able to be involved in the worship team, teach a Sunday-school class, host a small group Bible study, serve on committees, and more. In both cases, I was simply doing "what I could." Our circumstances change as we go through the passages of life. There will be times for all of us when we feel like we are accomplishing a great deal for God—and other times when we feel like we aren't making much of a difference outside our home and family. But I believe that God has much more empathy for us than we have for ourselves—and that He is asking us to do *what* we can *when* we can. Further, he asks us to do what only *we* can do.

ᘛᘚᘛᘚᘛ

Jesus was sharing a meal with His disciples and a motley crew of sinners in the home of Simon the leper when a woman came in, fell at his feet, and began to weep. She broke open a jar of costly fragrance and poured the entire contents on Jesus' head. The others in the room were indignant at her "wastefulness." Reacting, they said, "Why has this fragrant oil been wasted? For this oil might have been sold for more than 300 denarii and given to the poor" (Mark 14:4-5). Jesus' reply has become the cornerstone of my Christian service. He said, "Leave her alone. Why are you bothering her? She has done a noble thing for me...She has done what she could" (verses 6,8). And that, according to Jesus Himself, is what He expects. "Unto every one of us is given grace according to the measure of the gift of Christ" (Ephesians 4:7 KJV).

The Wilderness Is a Training Ground

Regardless of whether we believe God *sent* us to the wilderness or *allowed* us to go there, He does not want us to forget what we learned in that place. Have you ever been in a church at night and looked up at the stained-glass windows? They are pretty unimpressive. Almost dull. The lead ligature that holds the entire work together, hardly noticeable during daylight hours, is now more obvious than the glass, which appears dark and colorless at night. Stained glass requires light to bring it to life. So do we require Light to have life. Jesus, the light of the world, shines through our imperfect lives, shedding His light in us and through us to affect all those we touch. As with antique glass, our flaws are what make us unique as well as beautiful. Sadly, we spend more time hiding, masking, and denying our flaws than we do allowing His light to illuminate those flaws for His service.

In fact, antique stained glass is a fair representation of fragile humanity. European hand-blown stained glass comes in every color imaginable. It is riddled with color swirls and air bubbles and is of varying thickness. To make each pane, the artisan glass-maker uses a long blowpipe to blow gently into a swirled gather of molten, molasses-like glass. This viscous liquid is the result of sand being placed in a crucible and held in an 800-degree-Fahrenheit blast furnace until it melts. The *gather* is blown into a shape similar to a lady's muff. That shape is laid on its side on a flat surface. With one swift cut of a sharp blade, the cylinder of hot molten glass is sliced along one side, and the glass unfurls into a sheet.

Uniquely Flawed

Each completed sheet of antique-style stained glass is unique and can sell for as much as $700. Stained glass in the sheet has an impressive appearance of strength. But like humans, it is full of frailties. Within the body of the glass lie many hidden stresses and tensions, flaws and imperfections, and it is highly susceptible to fracture. I discovered this the hard way. While giving a lecture to a college class I carefully unwrapped a piece of antique glass, explaining its fragility in spite of its thickness. At that very moment, the piece of glass I was holding up in front of a window to illuminate its features slid from my hand. It shattered. My gasp of horror let the class know right away that this was not in the lesson plan!

I have a friend who studied stained-glass art at the Royal College of London. Half a lifetime later, she spent five years in intensive Bible study, prayer, and spiritual preparation before creating the five breathtaking stained-glass windows for the church we both attend. Every window has dozens of pieces, each painstakingly cut from sheets of antique glass she purchased in Europe. When her part of the project was complete, she brought all the pieces as well as the designs to a glazier so they could be leaded and framed. The glass had to be numbered so that the glazier would know which piece went where.

But the numbers could have blown off in a gust of wind and it would not have made any difference to her. Like Jesus the Shepherd, who calls His sheep by name, she knew each piece intimately. She knew each one by its flaws. She could have mixed up the whole lot and, like a jigsaw puzzle, sorted out and placed every piece in exactly the right spot. By virtue of their slight variance of color, of swirl, of bubbled surface, of ridges and contours, each piece was unique. Each had been lovingly and carefully chosen for one particular place. In just such a way, Jesus our Lord knows us intimately. And it is often our flaws that identify us. Those same flaws can provide you direction if, like I was, you are looking for "something to say."

Our Flaws Hold the Key to Our Calling

Instead of smoothing over our flaws, hiding them behind Sunday-morning masks, or denying they exist, I believe God wants us to study them for clues to our calling. Like many of you, I have done everything from teach Sunday school to play piano to sing to clean the building and set up chairs. Each of these areas of service is vital and necessary, and I have found pleasure and fulfillment in them. However, I began to sense that God was calling me on to something more difficult for me, more demanding of me. Something that would require more determination and courage from me. Something that would necessitate regular interaction with Him in order to accomplish it. Early in my faith walk, my first pastor, Henry Blackaby, taught me a valuable lesson, which he later wrote in *Experiencing God:*

> When God purposes to do something through you, the assignment will have God-sized dimensions. This is because God wants to reveal Himself to you and to those around you. If you can do the work in your own strength, people will not come to know God. However, if God works through you to do what only He can do, you and those around you will come to know Him.[1]

Had God called me to a public endeavor when I was smugly confident that I had plenty to say, I would not have had compassion for the broken drifter I was to become. So He waited until I was lost in the billowing sand on the backside of the desert before He said, "Therefore, go." He waited until I was no longer convinced He existed to call me to walk by faith in Him.

And what did He ask me to do? To be real, to admit I had been faking my faith for a long time, and to walk humbly with Him as He brought me out of the wilderness on the road to mature faith. Along the way I was to tell the truth, the same truth you've been reading in this book. In other words, He asked me to let His light shine through my unique, flawed fragility—to stand in the authenticity gap—so He could use my flaws to shed His light in a unique way.

Who better, for example, to help and encourage a recently separated man than another man who has already walked that road with God and grown closer to Him in the process? For another example, in the midst of the grief of losing a spouse or child, the empathy of a friend who has also known that deep hurt carries much weight. In the same way, I offer my wilderness journey as a testimony of hope to other wanderers. I've walked that dusty trail. I know how subtle Satan is and how easily he entraps us with lies about guilt and unworthiness that keep us wandering. I know the reality of self-protecting fear and how much work it is to learn to trust again. But I also know the God who "hounds" us and pursues us with relentless love in order to re-establish communication with us. I know that it is because of His persistence and my Spirit-empowered obedience that we can once again walk together in authentic faith.

Your Unique Shape Gives You a Unique Place

"God designed each of us so there would be no duplication in the world,"[2] comments Rick Warren. The reason stained-glass windows are beautiful is because every piece of glass is different. Every piece has flaws that reflect and refract the light in unique ways. The beauty comes from the contrast of different pieces in relationship together. If every piece looked the same, the result would not be as beautiful.

Finding our niche involves learning to accept ourselves for who we are, not for who we wish we were. My biggest insecurity when God called me to be a speaker was that I didn't think I had any credibility. I thought my wilderness disqualified me from that type of public service. Telling people I was a hypocritical faker who had worn a mask for years did not seem likely to inspire confidence in me or my message. On top of that, my natural ability lay in story-telling, not in biblical exegesis. It seemed to me that making people laugh by weaving tales was near the bottom of the list of necessary talents required for being on God's team. Teaching Scripture in a contemporary, dynamic style was where it was at, not storytelling, I thought. In short, I suffered from Beth Moore envy.

"Gift Envy"

Rick Warren cautions Christians about "gift envy." It is tempting to look at the gifts of others and wish we could be like that. What happens to those of us with gift envy? Insecurity and lack of confidence in our abilities join the swirling sandstorm of unbelief, and we wander in circles, unable to see our way, and accomplish nothing for Him. We are sidelined.

For the first year after my call to "go public," every time I prepared talks for a speaking engagement I went through a spell that lasted for hours or days in which I doubted my gifts and bemoaned the fact they were not like Beth Moore's. I would open the Scriptures and try to harvest deep truths—and in no time at all I would be miserable and discouraged. I had no insights, for the Word was still dead to me because I was battling unbelief and succumbing to crippling doubt.

In the midst of this trying season, I had been asked to speak at a weekend retreat in another province. I had, of course, agreed to this since that was the "deal" between God and me: If someone called, I would go. As I mentioned earlier, this obedience to go in the midst of my own debilitating doubt was to be my pathway out of the wilderness. But at that time, I was truly walking by faith because I did not feel "fixed" in any way. I also knew that my message, the only message I was qualified to give, had to be the truth about my wilderness trek. And so I began to prepare for the three talks I had to give.

As you can imagine, Satan was having a field day with me as I tried to put together my presentations. After two difficult days during which I made little progress, I got a call from one of my sisters. She was calling to thank me for the set of Beth Moore videos I had loaned her. When I told her I was preparing for a weekend speaking trip, she asked how it was going. "It's coming along okay," I lied. Sheesh! I couldn't even tell the truth to my sister—how was I supposed to tell the truth to the weekend group? My spirit sank even lower.

And then she said, "Is it going to be anything like Beth Moore's talks?" Before I had a chance to respond, my sister was off and running with praise for Beth's marvelous insights, her engaging style, her endearing vulnerability, and so on.

When she paused for breath, I croaked out my reply. "No, I don't think it'll be like that."

After more chitchat, we said our farewells. Although I knew my dear sis's remarks were entirely innocent and took no offense, the door to my soul was flung wide for spiritual attack. The next day was miserable as I once again faced my task and felt so completely inadequate. In desperation, after hours of fruitless attempts to prepare, I put on my shoes and went for a "slog"—my pitiful rendition of a slow jog. Slipping along on the muddy running path along the river, I called out to the still invisible, silent God for help.

And He met me there. He met me at the place I least expected but should have known He would. He met me at my point of need.

Just be yourself and tell the truth, I heard. Nothing fancy. No Scripture passages to go along with this celestial message. Just the comforting, guiding advice to do what I could. Like the woman who poured perfume on Jesus' feet did what she could, God was asking me to do no less. Not sure if these thoughts were His prompting or "self-talk," I decided, on faith, to risk that it was Him. And that weekend I spoke about my wilderness experience *and* my Beth Moore envy. And God, in His miraculous way, released me from the paralyzing grip of that envy as soon as I broke the conspiracy of silence and confessed it.

In the midst of feeling incredibly inadequate, completely unqualified, and dreadfully unspiritual, God was calling me to do the very thing He calls each of us to do—to do what I could. I could talk. I could go. I could tell the truth. What did I lack in order to fulfill that calling? Nothing. The enemy had seeded all those negative thoughts in his attempt to keep me silenced and useless.

Who Are You Now?

In case you are curious, God has since called me into deeper study of His Word. As I mentioned earlier, I have begun attending seminary classes and have increased my personal study time. What I am saying, though, is that at the time God called me to speak out for Him, none of that was happening in my life—but the call was still valid. He was asking me to be all I could be in that season, to use what I had to offer at that point. Remember, God's call is not dependent on our preparedness; it's dependent on our obedience.

Are you ever tempted to try to be someone else? To change your personal style because of a misplaced comment by a well-meaning person—even your spouse? To take singing lessons when you are suited for teaching? To teach when it is obvious to everyone else that your abilities are in administration? To study law when you are more apt to practice landscape design? God made you the way you are for a reason. *News flash:* Beth Moore can't reach everyone. Rick Warren can't reach everyone. Billy Graham can't reach everyone. Your pastor and mine can't reach everyone. And they would likely say the loudest amen to that. I had to learn to accept the fact that, when I did what I could, God would use me as a vehicle for His message of truth. My humor, as unspiritual as it seemed to me, could be sanctified for His service.

> Only you can be you…No one has the exact same mix of factors that make you unique. That means no one else on earth will ever be able to play the role God planned for you. If you don't make your unique contribution to the body of Christ, it won't be made. [3]

As long as I suffered from gift envy, I was paralyzed and ineffective. But God spoke clearly to me—He changed my wrong thinking. *Only you can be you, Connie. Whether you like who you are or not, I made you that way for a reason. If you don't be who you are— who I made you to be—My kingdom will be poorer.* When my thinking changed, the paralysis of fear loosed its hold, and I was able to do the job God had called me to do.

Charlene Ann Baumbich, inspirational speaker and author of both nonfiction and the hugely popular Dorothy Series, e-mailed me these helpful words during my season of learning to accept myself:

> 'Tis the humor that has opened all writing and speaking doors for me, even when I wasn't looking for doorways! One of the books I've written, *How to Eat Humble Pie Without Getting Indigestion,* is about being exactly who God created us to be. If He has given you the ministry of laughter (yes, that is how I see it), then make no apologies, lest you be apologizing for God seemingly making a mistake with you!
>
> I do not perceive myself to be a comedian, and I do make that distinction when people contact me. I

believe Christian comedians are wonderful and have their own ministry. For me the message is my ministry and humor is my vehicle. When we have laughed together we have shaken open a bit, become disarmed, and are more able to let in a message—even when it surprises us.

So be who you are and give thanks for the gift!

I take great solace in Walter Brueggemann's words: "The deep places in our lives—places of resistance and embrace—are not ultimately reached by instruction. Those places of resistance and embrace are reached only by stories, by images."[4] And so I go. I tell my stories. I share whatever God-given insights from the Word I can, and I trust Him to used my flawed fragility to radiate beautiful light to a hurting world.

> Whenever we are exactly who He created us to be and allow His light to beautify our flaws, we are part of His work in bringing mankind to faith in Christ.

Failure—A Great Qualification for the Job

David Roper's book *Jacob: The Fools God Chooses* uses stories to tell about all the imperfect characters God uses in His Story. His point is that God uses all of us, even fools like me, for His divine purposes. Failure does not disqualify us from ministry; it schools us. Chuck Colson says, "My greatest humiliation—being sent to prison—was the beginning of God's greatest use of my life; He chose the one experience in which I could not glory for His glory."[5] If failure disqualified us, the Bible would lose all its characters except for Jesus, the only sinless man.

Yet even though God permits failure in our lives He remains our advocate, praying that our faith will not fail. He will seek us out, as He did Jacob, shower us with His forgiveness, and *assure us that He has work for us to do.* "Oh, *felix culpa* [happy fault]," Augustine claimed, that makes us better than ever before.[6]

What kind of fool are you? Are you a dancing fool? Are you crazy for golf? Excited about scientific research? Nuts about decorating? Mad for hockey? Passionate about knitting booties? Artistic? Do you make a mean chili? Can you clean a car like no one else? What can you do? None of the things mentioned are listed in the Bible as spiritual gifts, yet all of them are as spiritual as we let them be. God is calling you, for He calls us all. You can simplify the whole process if you learn to accept yourself and then let Him use you in the manner in which you were designed. Anything we do, we do as unto Him—and He shines through our flaws, creating a masterpiece of beauty for His purposes. Whenever we are exactly who He created us to be and allow His light to beautify our flaws, we are part of His work in bringing mankind to faith in Christ.

A wonderful example of this comes from my own mother. When Gerry and I were married, he wore a black suit he had purchased for that occasion. Nine years later, when he was preparing to graduate from seminary with his master's degree, that was still his only suit—but the wide lapels were not in vogue any more. We couldn't afford another suit, so I called my mom, 2000 miles away, and asked for help. "If I sent you the suit, could you make the lapels narrower and bring it up to date?" I asked, hopeful.

She paused. I assumed she was mulling over the fact that I was asking her to spend hours on a difficult task that touched on an area still painful for her—our religious differences. "It's very hard to work on black fabric…and my eyesight isn't what it used to be," she began haltingly.

Hurt and confused about what to do next, I said the first thing that entered my head. "Do you know of anyone else in town who could do the job for a reasonable fee?" We lived in a high-end neighborhood in Marin County, California, where the cost of tailoring was out of my reach.

It was as though my mom "came to her senses." Quickly she said, "Send it to me. My machine is by the window. I'll do it on a sunny day."

I was caught off guard by her sudden about-face, so I stammered, "But…you don't have to do this. I know I'm asking a lot…"

"It's what I do," she said with finality. And the discussion was over. All my life, growing up, I had one enduring image of my mother—she was seated at her sewing machine. She truly spent hours every single day, sewing and mending clothes for her seven daughters and one son. She had trained as a young woman to become a seamstress, and years of practice had turned her into a professional tailor.

So when Mom said, "It's what I do," she was taking her humble position alongside the woman who poured costly perfume on Jesus' head. "She did what she could."

Our License to Serve

When God extends a hand to you in the wilderness and calls you to "therefore, go," don't turn your back on that call. Don't argue with Him and say He can't possibly use a sinner like you. "This is what the Lord says: If you return, I will restore you; you will stand in My presence. And if you speak noble [words], rather than worthless ones, you will be My spokesman" (Jeremiah

15:19). "Noble" words, you ask? "She has done a noble thing...She did what she could" (Mark 14:6,8). Through the uniqueness of our flawed life, we tell others the truth of His redemptive work. Our authenticity, our raw reality, our unique experience is our license to teach. What, in a nutshell, qualifies us for service?

A desire to know Him.

A willingness to forge ahead regardless of unbelief.

An obedient spirit.

A humbled, grateful heart.

A flawed life made beautiful by His light.

A determination to do what I can.

Peter, my soul mate and current favorite Bible guy, sees himself for who he really is and cries, "Go away from me, Lord, I am a sinful man" (Luke 5:8 NASB). But Jesus "didn't come to call the righteous, but sinners" (Mark 2:17). We are not worthy to serve based on who we are, we are worthy because of Who calls. He calls sinners. He calls flawed people. He calls wilderness wanderers. He calls those who have failed. He calls fakers.

No one is more grateful for that than me. Especially when I discovered that the call to ministry was actually a call to His presence. By responding to His call, I finally found what had eluded me for so long—an authentic relationship.

Nothing Else Satisfies

In my case, public speaking was an act of obedience I chose to do for many months before I sensed any touch from God's Spirit. In essence, *I was living by faith at a time when I thought I no longer had any.* Without even knowing it, I was applying the sweat equity of developing holy habits in the hope it would pay off. (See chapter 11.) And here is the crunch—if you are waiting to be "spiritual" enough before stepping forth, you'll be buried under desert sand. And you may get smothered and die there.

Our church elects deacon couples. The female half of one of these teams called me last night to ask a question. She was meeting a hurting person for coffee in a few moments, and she knew I had spent some time with that woman also. She called to ask if I had any helpful advice and to ask me to pray during the time they would meet. In closing, she mentioned she had almost refused the request to be part of a deacon couple because she was currently experiencing a season of dry faith. "I feel like I don't have anything to offer," she said.

I wanted to reach through the phone lines and grab her by the shoulders. "You are in the best possible position to help others," I fairly shouted, "because you know that without Him, you can do nothing." I paraphrased for her a quote from a book I was reading: The wanderer has "the awareness that you long to be someone you're not and cannot be without divine help."[7] Broken people help broken people. The woman she was meeting for coffee has suffered much betrayal and brokenness in her life. When we respond and reach out from the midst of our weakness, we display His power to heal, to transform, to redeem, to make a difference.

Once you have wandered in the wilderness of dry faith and have discovered that nothing satisfies—not materialism, not unfettered freedom, certainly not religious duty—you long to return to the heart of God. Like the writer of Ecclesiastes you have found that, without God, everything is meaningless. You yearn to see His hand at work and to hear His voice. Your deepest desire is to feel His smile and hear Him whisper, *Well done.* And He will do it. Risk praying a prayer of brokenness from a heart of little faith: *God, if You are real, and if You still love me, show Yourself to me. Tell me what to do and I will do it.* Then watch to see what happens "out of the blue."

∾∾∾

Soon after my public truth-telling began, God revealed to me
that the reason He wanted to speak "through" me was so He could
speak "to" me. Let me say this as plainly as I can. If calling you
forth is the only way God can re-establish a vital link with your
soul and reignite your hunger for Him, then He will do it. God
wants a relationship with you, His child. He will look for a way to
put you in the place you need Him most so that you must come
to Him. If I had not said *yes* to His call I might still be in the
wilderness. When I agreed to do something bigger than me,
something I could not do without His input, I was finally able to
get back on course. I have found that at the place I end, He begins.
Do you long for a mature faith? An authentic relationship with
the living God? If you are willing to be one of the "fools God
uses," He will meet you at that place and take you where He wants
you to be. He will give you "something to say."

CHAPTER FOURTEEN

The Personal God

O Jerusalem! Jerusalem!
The city who kills the prophets and
stones those who are sent to her!
How often I wanted to gather
your children together,
as a hen gathers her chicks under her wings,
but you were not willing!

Jesus

Just because God is silent
doesn't mean he's not active.

Gary Thomas

*K*irk and Laura established a pattern soon after they married in 1986. They would work hard, save their money, and then travel for up to two months a year. Kirk was the planner, and Laura was the "bean counter." The rest of the year they lived in Hawaii, where they pursued their passion for ocean surfing every day. An unusual Christmas present from Kirk's brother Rick in 1989 marked the beginning of a change in their life. The gift was a Bible.

Kirk was unimpressed. But when Rick's children exhibited more knowledge of the Bible than Kirk had, he was embarrassed.

Considering himself well read, and certainly well educated, he decided to find out what was in this most famous of all books. Rick suggested he begin with the book of John.

Every day at sunset, a spiritual time of day in Hawaii, when it got too dark to surf, Kirk and Laura would sprawl on the living-room floor and read one chapter of John. Only one. Then they recited in unison the only prayer they knew—the Lord's Prayer. "We were still partying to the max," Kirk says. "But we were seeking. We had no church. My brother had returned to Oregon. We were alone. I read the Bible like a fable. I liked Jesus. He was a champion of the underdog. I began to put my hope in Christ, but I couldn't articulate it."

෪ ෪ ෪

These late-afternoon times became the high point of the couple's day, and they looked forward to them. Every day was a new adventure as they followed the life of Jesus with growing interest and curiosity. It was hard to limit their reading to one chapter, but they did. Then, 19 days into this new spiritual quest, Kirk read about the crucifixion of his new hero. He couldn't believe it. "My heart was broken," he recalls, tears running down his face as he recounts the story 13 years later. "It was like the color had drained out of my world." He felt tricked. "I didn't want to read John any more."

Kirk's despair robbed him of energy. He dragged himself listlessly through his routine tasks for a few days. Only God knows—and I mean that—what compelled Kirk to pick up his Bible again at sunset some days later. In chapter 20, he read,

> On the first day of the week Mary Magdalene came to the tomb early, while it was still dark. She saw that the stone had been removed from the tomb. So she ran to

Simon Peter and to the other disciple, whom Jesus loved, and said to them, "They have taken the Lord out of the tomb, and we don't know where they have put Him!" (John 20:1-2).

"I couldn't read fast enough," Kirk remembers. When Mary tells Peter and John about the empty tomb, they run to see for themselves. It was open and empty just as she had reported. Not finding Jesus or anyone else there to explain what had happened, the two disciples returned home. But Mary hung around, and her waiting was rewarded. She was the first one to see the risen Christ. Do you not think it is significant that Jesus chose Mary to be the first one? Mary, who had more baggage than a camel train, has the honor of being the one chosen to tell the others He was alive.

> Mary stood outside facing the tomb, crying. As she was crying, she stooped to look into the tomb. She saw two angels in white sitting there, one at the head and one at the feet, where Jesus' body had been lying. They said to her, "Woman, why are you crying?"
>
> "Because they've taken away my Lord," she told them, "and I don't know where they've put Him." Having said this, she turned around and saw Jesus standing there, though she did not know it was Jesus.
>
> "Woman," Jesus said to her, "why are you crying? Who is it you are looking for?"
>
> Supposing He was the gardener, she replied, "Sir, if you've removed Him, tell me where you've put Him, and I will take Him away."
>
> "Mary!" Jesus said.
>
> Turning around, she said to Him in Hebrew, "Rabbouni!"—which means "Teacher" (verses 11-16).

"If He's alive, that changes everything!" Kirk shouted. "I felt like my team had won the Super Bowl! At that moment, I was born again."[1]

It was not Kirk's brother Rick, a neighbor, a pastor, or anyone else who forged this supernatural, spiritual union. It was God who revealed Himself to Kirk through His Word.

The Touch of His Hand

God is personal. He seeks us. He finds us. He calls us to Himself. I can only speak for myself—and I do not suggest my experience reflects anyone else's—but spiritual encounters like these are rare for me. So infrequent that when it happens, it's huge. The first time I really "saw" God was the day I chose to become a Christ-follower in 1973. As with Kirk, there was a moment when I knew His Spirit had arrived. I knew I was different. Almost 30 years later, after spending a decade in the wilderness of dry faith, I sensed God's presence again in a similar way, and it was a turning point.

This encounter took place when I spoke a third time with a message from Psalm 51. Twice already at Restoring Joy conferences, in two other provinces, I had told the truth about my years of wilderness wandering. Some women had privately told me they'd needed to hear what I'd said. It gave them hope. This third event was in my home province. This audience knew me. They had walked with me, taught Sunday school with me, participated in the same events, played in the same worship band—we shared the same religious community. And for years I had been faking it, pretending to have an active relationship with the living God when my life was just empty works.

Driving to that conference, I was quiet and subdued. I did not want to face my friends with the confession I had to make. I called out to God for help; I heard nothing. I knew I had to tell the truth, because why else would He have orchestrated this experience? He had finally given me "something to say." It just so happened I wasn't too keen on saying it to this group of women!

With a heavy heart, in the final meeting I spoke of my long sojourn in the wilderness of dry faith. The crowd that had laughed uproariously through the other sessions sat silent. Here and there I saw tears trickle down faces. I definitely had my listeners' attention, but I was not comfortable with it. All my life, I had used my ability to make people laugh to lighten moments of tension—and suddenly, there was absolutely nothing funny I could say.

The event organizer asked me to extend an altar call after my final talk. As if I wasn't already a nervous wreck! I had seen pastors give invitations for 30 years, but I had never had to do it myself and was completely intimidated by the request. What really scared me was not "What if no one comes?" I was scared someone *would* respond. I was in no condition to give spiritual counsel.

∽∾∽

At the end of the talk, I asked the worship leader to play the keyboard quietly. Everyone bowed their heads and closed their eyes. I invited the women to come forward for prayer or counsel. I stumbled over my words. Nobody moved. I ran out of "come-on-down" things to say, and I bowed my head too. The room was still except for the soft music behind me. At that moment, I sensed that God wanted me to go kneel at the base of the platform. I don't say I heard a voice; it was more like a nudge, a spiritual push. Already humiliated, I had nothing left to lose. I abandoned the podium and the bewildered worship leader who, thankfully, kept playing. I descended the few stairs, knelt alone at the bottom, and shook with silent sobs. And at that moment, He came to me.

I heard Him this time. Clearly. I heard Him say something that to this day still surprises me, moves me, and fills me with wonder. After my decade of wilderness wandering, I thought I had forever forsaken the possibility I might please God again. But in that moment of brokenness He placed His warm hand on my right shoulder—I felt it—and whispered tenderly in my ear, *Well done.* It was that unmistakable still, small voice I had once known. Like the Children of Israel after crossing the Jordan river on dry land, I put up a spiritual marker. I will forever look to that symbolic stone pile dubbed "well done" with deep gratitude for His personal touch.

> The sacrifices of God are a broken spirit; a broken and contrite heart, O God, thou wilt not despise (Psalm 51:17 KJV).

How true. I was broken: humiliated before my friends, humbled before my God. I was contrite: sorry for wandering into the wilderness and sorry for staying there so long. And He did not despise me. On the contrary, He affirmed me. He pursued me. He came to me personally to say, *Well done.* The women at this conference reacted the same way others had. Publicly, they thanked me for my humorous stories. Privately, some came to me with tears and admitted they were also wanderers.

Waiting Expectantly

That personal touch from God provided a glimpse of what could be, a glimpse of the relationship I had once known and somehow drifted from. I would ride on that experience for a long time. I would have to. Although He met me there at my point of need, my sense of His realness would not become a daily reality for a long time. I'm still journeying with Him to that place I believe by faith exists, the place where I am infused and empowered by a moment-by-moment sense of His presence. Although I read my Bible daily and pray, He doesn't speak to me each day. Or is it that I don't hear Him? Probably so. But I take great comfort in knowing I will hear from Him again before long.

I understand now that my role is to be obedient.

> The problem is not that God is distant and needs to be wooed or badgered into coming near; the problem is that God is ever present, ever near, and that some of us seek ways of escape...God does not need to be invoked, we do. We need to be called to our senses, to be as present to God as God is to us. To stop running. To stand still, breathe in.[2]

And so, Bible open before me each day, I expectantly approach Him. And wait. Sometimes I see Him, sometimes I don't. After reading Scripture this morning, I wrote in my journal, "You did not speak to me through Your Word today. But that's okay. I'm going on faith that somehow, some way, You will intercept my life today. I will look for You."

I speak out of my experience to people like me, people who need hope. Sinners who want to know a personal God. Broken people. Imperfect people. Flawed, fragile people. Real people. Try-again people. Give-me-another-chance people. Whoops-I-did-it-again people. Is that who you are? Don't give up.

You Have a Friend

Performance-based religious service is crippling Christians and emptying our churches. Jesus gave everything, forsaking heaven—for what? Because He loved the Father. "Wasn't it because He loved me," you ask? Yes, Jesus died on my behalf, of course. But He died *because* it was the Father's plan. He endured the cross because of His love relationship with God the Father. That was His primary motivation and what sustained Him throughout His hideous ordeal.

And that same love relationship is what God desires to have with each one of us. He wants it more than He wants your wonderful singing, or preaching, or telling, or going. He wants you to love Him and to know the depth of His love for you. Who among us would die for a stranger? Yet most of us would die for our children. Why? Because we love them more than we love our own life. That's the type of love available to us in relationship with the Father. That's what motivates us to serve, to tell, to go. Anything less is empty works. It drains us and makes us bitter. It makes us resent the church and all the jobs we do there. It burns us out and leaves us casualties. It keeps us from talking about Jesus with our friends. Why would we tell our friends the "good news" when it is so burdensome to us?

"Jesus is the uncontested delight of my life," Beth Moore writes:

> I never intended for this to happen. I didn't even know it was possible. It all started with an in-depth study of His word in my late twenties and then surged oddly enough with a near emotional and mental collapse in my early thirties. At the end of myself I came to the beginning of an intensity of relationship with an invisible Savior.[3]

In brokenness we finally see clearly. We see who we are. And who He is. Once that happens, the Father can meet us on a personal level and take us to places we can't go on our own. "The dark night begins at the point at which we end, where our will and abilities are no longer enough to get us by, and God begins."[4]

Who's Your God?

So many of us don't know who God really is. Unknowingly, we follow false gods. The danger inherent in "getting rid of your God," like Lynne Hybels did in chapter 4, is that you replace Him with another false god. A god very prevalent in North American evangelical churches today is the Santa-god. His job is to satisfy our needs and most of our wants, and occasionally throw in a pleasant surprise as a bonus. All we have to do is to be a good girl or boy all year long, and Santa-god will give us all the stuff on our list. I suspect this faulty thinking is a cultural message we absorb simply by living in the me-centered world of North American affluence.

Everywhere we look we hear messages like "because you're worth it"; "you deserve a break today." Because many believers do not read their Bible during the week or attend Bible studies, the only time they hear a God-centered message is on Sunday morning. A 30-minute sermon once a week must compete with the round-the-clock advertising barrage from television, Internet, movies, radio, and the morning paper, all telling us how great we are and that we should not settle for less than the best—because we really do deserve it.

And it's not just the media—our peers send us messages that can confuse and mislead us. Something wonderful happens to us, whether it's a surprise Christmas bonus from the boss or that our house sells for more than we're asking, and our peers slap us on the back and say, "Congratulations! It couldn't happen to a nicer guy. You deserve it."

Do we deserve it? Why would I deserve a bonus or a lucrative house sale while others cling to the high branches of a tree as their houses are carried away in a flood before their very eyes? Why would I deserve any of the comforts I enjoy while AIDS makes millions of children orphans in Africa? Wizened grannies are raising a dozen hungry grandchildren because the generation between them has been wiped out. I have not yet figured out a polite response to the well-meaning friend who congratulates me for a bit of "good fortune." But the truth is, I don't deserve it. Neither do you. Don't ever fall into the trap of entitlement, because the moment you do, your relationship with God grows stale.

Without realizing it, in the years following my conversion, I allowed the messages of Western culture to infuse my thinking. (We wear our culture like a nicotine patch—it seeps into our system, changing the way we feel without our conscious notice. No need to inhale!) I came to believe that happiness was my right. And the pursuit of happiness became my goal. Unless we are students of history, we are unaware of how culture has changed over the last two generations. When my parents grew up in the first half of the last century, they were taught to be good. To live with honor. To do the right thing. That's why, before the draft began, thousands of Canadian men volunteered to fight to help save Europe from the Nazi invasion in 1939. Happiness, if it came at all, would simply be a by-product of right living.

During my upbringing, that message had already started to shift. Last century's call for North Americans to live with honor and integrity evolved into a self-centered pursuit of me-comforts that continues on into the new millennium. Nowadays, parents knock themselves out trying to ensure their children grow up happy. This "happiness" consists of padding their world with creature comforts that have all the staying power of a fruit diet for an elite athlete. We have absorbed and are passing on to our children the gospel of entitlement: "God loves you, and you deserve to be happy. Here's my credit card. Go crazy!"

A Man of Integrity Who Knew God

Dr. Darrell Osborne, who was born in 1919 (the same year as my own dad), exhibited with his life exactly what I am talking about in regard to the cultural shift that happened between my parents' generation and mine. Like my parents, Darrell was raised to "be good." He learned early on that life was hard and that he was expected to work hard and do the right thing…and that happiness, if it came at all, would be a by-product.

And he did work hard. He studied medicine and became an OB-GYN. He, along with his wife, Dorothy, set up practice in Kamloops, British Columbia, and stayed for 25 years. During those years, he was often heard to say he had never been happier.

Darrell become a Christ follower at the age of 32 and worked as hard in the church as he did in his practice. When he was 55 years old and "at the top of his game" he left his life in Canada and his five grown children, and he and Dorothy became medical missionaries at the Eku Baptist Hospital in Eku, Nigeria. Dorothy, who had a master's degree in social work, taught psychology and sociology at the nursing school there, and Darrell did everything imaginable in the medical field because the need was so great for doctors.

During his tenure in Eku, Darrell said he had never worked so hard or been so exhausted or so often ill. He had dengue fever (also called "breakbone fever" because of how painful it is), as well as hepatitis twice and malaria several times. He worked from sunup to sundown and sometimes was called during the night.

And again he said he had never been happier or more fulfilled in his work than he was in Nigeria.

"Happiness was a continuum for Darrell, and those years at Eku were some of the happiest of our lives," Dorothy told me, speaking for her husband, who passed away in 2000. What made that experience happy? "Just living in obedience to God's call—we were so thankful for the experiences we had, the people we met and grew to love," she said. "I never heard Darrell complain, not when he was ill or even when he was shot at and his car was stolen! He was doing what he loved to do, and he believed he was making a difference. That was enough."

To Know Him As He Is

The apostle Paul had no illusions that life should be easy or happy. He clearly understood that "it's not about me and my happiness."

> Everything that was a gain to me, I have considered to be a loss because of Christ. More than that, I also consider everything to be a loss in view of the surpassing value of knowing Christ Jesus my Lord. Because of Him I have suffered the loss of all things and consider them filth, so that I may gain Christ and be found in Him...My goal is to know Him and the power of His resurrection and the fellowship of His sufferings (Philippians 3:7-10).

Paul experienced the true meaning of life. Forsaking the status and comforts he once enjoyed as a Pharisee, he joyfully embraced suffering. For what reason? To know Christ. Paul tells us, and he has the scars to back it up, that real life is lived from the inside out, not the outside in.

However, in the life lived outside in, there's no room for pain. Pain seldom makes us happy, so we look for ways to get around it. Unlike Paul, we do not wish to know "the fellowship of His suffering." Pain avoidance is what drives the megabillion-buck pharmaceutical industry. Whether it is the pain of depression, or fatigue, or aching muscles, or sore joints, we look for ways to medicate ourselves so we don't have to feel it.

Now don't slam the book shut—I take pills too! I don't like headaches either. And I am not talking about people who suffer from afflictions over which they have no control—we are all thankful for modern medicine that eases the suffering of arthritics and allows others with chronic conditions to lead a more normal life. Most of my pain comes as a result of poor choices. Too much caffeine, too little sleep, and too much time looking at a computer screen can make my head hurt and my vision blur. There are two ways to "fix" this problem: drink another cup and keep working, or take a break and get some exercise. I don't always choose the healthier option.

Santa-god is supposed to bring us happiness and keep us from pain if we are good little girls and boys. Sounds nice, doesn't it? Too bad it doesn't work. The reason we wind up in the wilderness is because Santa-god theology—what too many of us believe without even realizing it—doesn't work. When life bites, Santa-god can't help. That is why the wilderness is a good place; it is a necessary place. It is where we forge a faith that will work in the real world. It is a place to recognize our flawed theology and to slay the Santa-god. It is a place to find the *real* God. It's where we admit our weakness and learn to rely on His strength. Mature faith will not crumble in the face of tragedy, betrayal, suffering, illness, grief, or loss. Mature faith rises out of the ashes of brokenness.

Who Is the Real God?

> Let me set this before you as plainly as I can. If a person climbs over or through the fence of a sheep pen instead of going through the gate, you know he's up to no good—a sheep rustler! The shepherd walks right up to the gate. The gatekeeper opens the gate to him and the sheep recognize his voice. He calls his own sheep by name and leads them out. When he gets them all out, he leads them and they follow because they are familiar with his voice (John 10:1-4 MSG).

The real God knows us personally. He is our Shepherd, and He calls us by name. We hear His voice, recognize it, and follow.

The problem is, the wilderness wanderer has forgotten what that voice sounds like. Worse yet, he assumes the Voice is no longer there. The wanderer feels abandoned, perhaps fearing that the Voice was never real, only a myth. But God, like the shepherd who goes out in search of one lost sheep (see Luke 15:1-7), is a God who pursues His children. "If we are faithless, He remains faithful, for He cannot deny Himself" (2 Timothy 2:13). He calls them to Himself. His desire is that we know Him personally, as sheep know their shepherd.

In biblical times, and still today in many countries, shepherds care for and live with their flock. Leading them by day to open pasture and calm water, the shepherds often enclose their sheep in a stone-walled pen at night to protect them from predators. That way, the shepherds can rest easy, sharing the watch with others so that the sheep are never left unguarded. In the morning, when it is time to leave the penned area and head out to pasture, each shepherd goes to the gate and calls his sheep. Only those sheep that have been raised hearing the distinctive sound of that voice will respond and go near him. The others will shy away in fear.

So too do we learn to recognize the voice of a personal God. When He calls and we think we hear, we obey by faith. He gives us assurances that it was His voice and that He is pleased with our obedience. He calls again. We obey again. He reassures us. This is the relationship between God and a new believer. Slowly, over time, we learn to hear His voice and see His hand in the affairs of our lives. The invisible God becomes visible. He becomes personal. We learn to trust our instincts, and following Him becomes easier. This needs qualifying—what He calls us to is not easier, but discerning His voice becomes less difficult.

When Will It Get Easier?

Here's where we run into trouble. Just as we can operate under the delusion that we'll someday become sinless (see chapter 8), a misconception we can have about the Christian life is that it should get easier over time. So when we encounter trials, difficulties, tragedies, and storms, it knocks some of us off course. And we begin to drift. We weren't expecting trouble. We didn't sign on for pain.

What we forget is that there is a thief. And he comes only "to steal and to kill and to destroy" (John 10:10). God promises us life to the full in the second half of that verse, but "there's an Enemy in your life with a different agenda," writes John Eldredge. "We are at war."[5] Instead of recognizing the enemy for who he is, we begin to be afraid of God. "Why would God let my daughter be molested while I was serving Him on a missions trip?" "Why would the church van full of college students en route to a weekend retreat be struck by a semi, killing all on board?" "Why would a plane carrying the leaders of three major mission agencies crash, leaving no survivors?" When tragedy strikes, instead of recognizing the hand of the enemy, we blame God for not preventing it.

In the midst of the pain of our suffering and our unanswered questions He continues to call, but we are paralyzed by fear because we feel tricked. *Why didn't God stop the accident, protect my child, rescue the passengers?* He strides on ahead of us, wanting to lead—but we can no longer follow because we have lost sight of Him in the sandstorm of our fear. The more this happens, the less we know Him. The more unfamiliar His voice becomes, the more we doubt His existence. Eventually, we wouldn't recognize Him if He walked up to our table and tried to take our order.

Staying Connected

Jesus' illustration of the vine and the branches is unparalleled in its simplicity for helping us understand our role as believers.

> I am the true vine, and My Father is the vineyard keeper. Every branch in Me that does not produce fruit He removes, and He prunes every branch that produces fruit so that it will produce more fruit. You are already clean because of the word I have spoken to you. Remain in Me, and I in you. Just as a branch is unable to produce fruit by itself unless it remains on the vine, so neither can you unless you remain in Me (John 15:1-4).

Jesus tells us we are *already clean*. In other words, if we have chosen to become a Christ-follower, we have everything we need. However, our lives will be ineffective, will not produce fruit, if we lose our connection.

Five times, Jesus says, "Remain."

I am the vine; you are the branches. The one who remains in Me and I in him produces much fruit, because you can do nothing without Me. If anyone does not remain in Me, he is thrown aside like a branch and he withers. They gather them, throw them into the fire, and they are burned (verses 5-6).

What does He mean by "remain"? Stay connected! He doesn't say, "Get connected," because the believer already *is* connected. *Remain!* Just stay there, for goodness' sake! What happens to the branch that loses its connection? It withers. It dries up. The wilderness of *dry* faith is where you find wanderers who have lost their connection. They haven't lost their salvation, just their connection. God is ready, at a moment's notice, to graft us back into His Vine.

He doesn't say, "Get connected,"
because the believer already *is* connected. *Remain!*
Just stay there, for goodness' sake!

Picking Up His Signals

How do we get reconnected to the Vine? A new believer in a church in Ontario described her experience of coming to know the Lord this way: "We are all born with satellite dishes on our heads. But until we come to know Jesus in a personal way, we are never pointed in the right direction, so we don't pick up His signals. Once we know Him, He adjusts our dish, and we begin to get the message clearly for the first time!"[6]

Just to save a few bucks, last year Gerry decided to risk his life on our steep, slippery roof in winter and install our first satellite dish. He learned right away—as the Chinook wind howled down from the Rocky Mountains, threatening to blow him straight to

Abraham's bosom—that close isn't good enough. It has to be exact. The dish has to be tilted at exactly the right angle in the right direction in order for it to receive the signal. Using his cell phone to speak to one of our kids, who was watching the television screen for reception, Gerry would make a tiny adjustment and then ask, "Anything yet?"

"Not yet, Dad."

When he finally got it right, he didn't need the cell phone to hear the mighty cheer that arose from the kid, who was sick to death of watching a blank screen!

∽∽∽

Wanderers are people whose "dish" is pointing in the wrong direction. We're picking up the enemy's signal because we are worshiping a false god—Santa-god. We need to get pointed in the right direction. Without wanting to beat this thing to death, may I say that, even when our dish is not getting the right signal, the Signal-Sender is still there! He hasn't gone anywhere. He's waiting for the dish to be properly aligned. Where this illustration falls apart is, unlike the signal that passively waits to be picked up, God *pursues* us in our wilderness, looking for ways to help us reconnect.

The adjustment you need to make so you can once again hear God is to stop blaming God for Satan's work—and believe, on faith, that God loves you and wants a personal relationship with you. And then wait. If you hear that still, small voice, gratefully accept it as His personal touch. Don't expect the floodgates of communication to open. You didn't wander into the wilderness overnight—you won't find your way out after one day's march. But take comfort in the fact that you are pointing in the right direction.

CHAPTER FIFTEEN

In Whom We Trust

In God I trust; I will not fear.
What can man do to me?
King David

It is impossible to go through life without trust:
That is to be imprisoned in the worst cell of all, oneself.
Graham Greene, *The Ministry of Fear*

*A*nne is a dead ringer for Liza Minnelli, with her huge eyes, impish grin, and zany, faddish hairstyles. Talking a mile a minute while blinking the bangs out of her eyes with a thick wedge of dark lashes, she makes friends easily. She fell in love early and married her sweetheart. She had an active relationship with Christ and was thrilled to be serving God by using her relational gifts. A natural evangelist, she was legendary for leading others to faith in Christ. Few could resist the effects of her vibrant faith and bubbly personality.

The day Anne discovered that her church's associate pastor, a close family friend, had sexually abused one of her children, her world was soundly rocked for the first time. The entire church was thrown into a period of such grief and devastation that she feared it would split wide open and never recover. Anne's heart was severely wounded, and in her frustration and pain, she was consumed by an anger that shocked her with its ferocity. She knew anger was the natural response of a mother when one of her children is hurt, but she kept waiting for God to give her the supernatural response of love and forgiveness. It never came.

She began to drift spiritually. She lost her focus and stopped telling others about Jesus. Her Bible lost its power to comfort and sustain her. The family moved to another city, a new job, and a new church. Anne did less and less in the church and found new satisfaction in a sales career at which she excelled.

And then another crisis occurred. Worse than the first one. She didn't know if she would recover this time. Her trust in her husband, her lover, her best friend, was shattered. She reeled in shock—the pain felt like a knife wound to the chest that threatened to kill her, she said. At her lowest point, while on a shopping trip with some friends, she collapsed alone in the stairwell of a mall and sobbed her heart out. She railed at God for this latest assault. Why had He allowed this to happen? Didn't He love her anymore? Unable to sleep, falling behind at work, and trying to act normal in front of the children all took their toll. She reached the end of her strength and moved out. She parked her suitcase in a friend's basement and crawled into a borrowed bed.

"I just needed to rest," Anne said, explaining why she had felt the need to leave her family. "All I did was cry all day and night, and I needed to get away to a quiet place where I could sleep." During this time of separation, she would have to decide whether or not her marriage was worth saving. She had never been so confused or in so much pain. Everyone and everything she had trusted in seemed to have let her down.

༺ ༻ ༺

This was the state of things for Anne—estranged from her husband and disappointed with God—the night she heard me tearfully share the truth about my journey into the wilderness of dry faith at a weekend retreat. After I spoke, the worship leader invited people to personally encounter their Lord as the musicians quietly played. Anne fell to the floor, pushing chairs aside as she went down. There she lay, prostrate between the jumble of chairs and trouser legs, weeping in the agony of a broken heart. Others gathered around, praying, as her pain came out in sobs no words could express.

That was a pivotal moment for Anne. What connected with her wounded heart was hearing the truth about someone else's wilderness journey. Suddenly she didn't feel so alone, so abandoned, so guilty for drifting away. God used that truth to show her she could be set free from the prison of hurt and fear. She and her husband reconciled. She moved back home, returned to church, and began the journey of recovery.

It was a beginning. But she had many more miles to go. She wanted to go back to the good old days of her relationship with the Lord, where she had sensed His presence and peace—but she didn't know how to get there. Could she trust Him again? Even though her marriage was on the mend, she still wandered in the wilderness of doubt and disappointment.

Anne was singing along with the worship band on a Sunday morning several months hence when she sensed God speaking to her. It had been a long time since she'd discerned His voice, so at first she wasn't sure how to respond. She hesitated and kept singing. But then she heard it again. God was using the words of the song to speak directly to her. *Turn around*, she sang and heard simultaneously.

She suddenly realized that, ever since suffering the shock of hearing that a trusted friend had abused her child, she had been looking back—in anger—to that day. Her inability to look ahead had crippled her and thrust her into a place of paralyzing fear, where she had remained, almost to the point of losing her faith. But as she sang she heard God say, *Turn around. Look ahead. Take your eyes off the past, and you will see Me again.* It was a freeing moment, a moment of revelation and release. Anne realized that in order to grow, she must look ahead and leave the past behind. The truth that Jesus leads us like a shepherd leads his sheep—out in front—swept over her in a fresh way.

Part of a song Anne wrote in the following days reflects her experience that God pursues us like a lover, calls us into personal communion, and wants to free us with His truth:

Your whispers of love—they found me
Your grace soothed the pain of my past
Your glory warmed my upturned face
Your hand was on the small of my back

Anne and some friends have formed an outreach through which they offer intimate weekend gatherings that allow women to tell the truth about their deepest hurts and hear the truth about the Father's deep love. Anne's life is a beautiful example of God's redemptive alchemy, which turns the ashes of personal disappointment into the gold of His healing presence.

We Are to Fear God but Not Be Afraid of Him

A truth that cannot be denied is that *life hurts*. I have never met an adult who has not experienced the pain of disappointment, loss, heartbreak, or betrayal. Because words are always inadequate, let me make a play on words to get the point across. We are to fear God but not be afraid of Him. Jesus tells us, "Don't fear those who kill the body but are not able to kill the soul; but rather, fear Him who is able to destroy both soul and body in hell" (Matthew 10:28). This kind of fear is a holy reverence. Recognize that no matter what "man" does to us, it is God alone who decides our destiny—and eternal destination. "Humility should be a hallmark of those who fear God. To accept that God's ways are often mysterious, that His wisdom is infinite and ours only finite, is an important expression of humility."[1]

Jesus continues,

> Aren't two sparrows sold for a penny? Yet not one of them falls to the ground without your Father's consent. But even the hairs of your head have all been counted. Don't be afraid therefore; you are worth more than many sparrows (Matthew 10:29-31).

In other words, fear God, respect Him for who He is—but don't be afraid of Him, for He loves you with an everlasting love. Although He is righteous and will decide our future based upon our present choices, He loves us. He loves us much more than He loves a bunch of pesky birds, and He wants to guide us into all truth so we may fully know His love. He is working to give us a mature faith—to conform us "to the likeness of his Son" (Romans 8:29 NIV).

Many days I am still afraid of God; I still believe in Santa-god even though I desperately want to know the real God. Whenever I hear stories from Christian friends about their ongoing, unresolved heartache with a child, or spouse, or circumstance, it scares me. It removes the cloak of false confidence in religious works I sometimes still wear as a protective mantle. It leaves me naked and vulnerable. It takes away all guarantees and the house-of-cards hope that helps me sleep nights as I foolishly do the math of my good-girl life and hope Santa-god is keeping score.

I still catch myself wanting to bargain with Santa-god. I send promises heavenward that I'll be really, really good from now on if He will just protect me and my children from unthinkable circumstances. Every day I give God a new opportunity to exercise patience with my childish faith. I want an adult faith, but the price tag still scares me some days. I want to know the real God, but I often lack the courage to fully trust Him.

Speaking about the apostle John's words in 1 John 2:12-14, "Robert Kysar helpfully proposes that we understand three stages in John's concept of faith—an embryonic stage that is at least open to faith (which is required before God will grant any sign), preliminary faith based on signs, and a mature faith that no longer requires them."[2] Somewhere in that territory between what Kysar calls preliminary faith and mature faith, I wandered into the wilderness of dry faith. Unconsciously wanting to remain in spiritual childhood, I was still relying on God to send me constant, doting signs of His love.

Looking Ahead with Trust

When we lived in California we became friends with a Christian named Sam. He was a few years older than Gerry. His erect posture, lean physique, and disciplined lifestyle all bore witness to his military background. However, he wore the evidence of his former career with the casualness of a sweater flung over one's shoulders. Stiff he wasn't. He oozed a relaxed charm, displayed an affable nature.

Sam had been a U.S. Navy SEAL—an elite corps of maritime

warriors—and had served in Vietnam. On his tours of duty, he had spent hours slogging through waist-high swamps, never knowing if a sniper would spy him or a poisonous snake would get the job done first and save the bullet. He knew real fear. Fear you could taste. Fear that made you shiver in the steamy climate. Fear that shadowed him night after night, day after day, for months on end. By the time we knew Sam, Vietnam was more than a decade behind him but, as for most vets, the images were still vivid.

One day as Sam and my husband drove along the California freeway en route to a conference, Gerry confessed he sometimes was afraid of God. That God sometimes asked him to do some hard things, and he was more than a little worried about God's latest request. Gerry had just been offered a bilingual position in Quebec and was afraid that his French, unused since childhood, wouldn't be strong enough to meet this challenge.

"Don't be afraid of God," Sam blurted out, and burst into tears. "Don't ever be afraid of God!" Sam begged Gerry to understand who God really is. Life will scare us, but it is God who walks with us through the terror of our circumstances. Sam had a mature faith, a seasoned relationship with the same God who had sacrificed His own dear Son. Sam knew what God was really like—he had a faith and trust that had been forged in the horrors of days dodging enemy bullets and nights sleeping with one eye open and his hand on his gun.

Sharing our future with God is all about looking ahead with trust. As long as we continue to look over our shoulder in fear at pain or betrayal, we'll never experience the freeing truth of God's love. Sharing our future with God may require that we walk through a season of pain. None of us want to experience pain, but that is the only road to mature faith. I have yet to meet anyone, Christian or otherwise, who has had a pain-free life.

Pushing Through the Pain

Children are brought forth in pain. "'I will intensify your labor pains,' God said to Eve, 'you will bear children in anguish'" (Genesis 3:16). Nowadays it is normal for dads to share the childbirth experience. It has not always been so. In 1980 in rural Saskatchewan when we were expecting our first child, it was uncommon for men to be in the delivery room. I wanted Gerry with me, but I was smugly convinced he wouldn't be able to handle it. We were told that in order for him to get delivery-room clearance he had to view a childbirth film. Medical professionals used this film as a filter for queasy dads; if Pop survived the film, he was in.

I had already read several books on natural childbirth, practiced breathing, and confidently told my doctor I wanted no pharmaceutical or surgical intervention of any kind. With a cockiness bred from ignorance, I thought I was ready. But I wasn't too sure about Gerry. I decided to go along with him to view the film just in case he needed a hand to hold. We arrived at the Public Health office with two little bags of homemade popcorn.

By this time I was past eight months, large and uncomfortable, and needing assistance to rise from low couches. I lumbered in, and we sat down on two straight-backed wooden chairs in a room smaller than most bathrooms. The screen covered one entire wall; we had front-row seats.

The nurse doused the lights and started the film. The larger-than-life characters were right in our face. I opened my popcorn and began to nibble, wondering how Gerry would react when things got dicey. I peeked sideways. He was also nibbling and showed no signs of discomfort.

The film star was blonde, cheerful, in peak condition, and uninhibited. We watched as she arrived at the hospital with her little suitcase in one hand, her little husband holding the other.

Every few hours, we would revisit the birthing room to see how she was progressing. On film, this took only minutes, giving the impression that labor is a quick, painless affair. What we didn't know was that they were saving celluloid for the really grisly parts. Eventually the mildly panting mama was wheeled into the delivery room looking fresh as a daisy. I peered sideways to see how Gerry was doing. This was, after all, a test to see if he would pass out during delivery. He had an intense look of concentration on his face. And was that a smile? It was too dark to tell.

The expectant momma began to push, and the camera zoomed in on the action. I started to feel a little queasy. There's a reason I never pursued a career in any facet of medicine; I faint at the sight of blood. Suddenly, without any warning whatsoever, the doctor—who from my vantage point was nine feet tall and as wide as a bus—asked the nurse for a needle. A close-up shot revealed a device the size of a javelin. The last thing I heard was the doctor asking for a scalpel. I felt betrayed. I expected childbirth, not butchery!

The lights went out all over the world. I slumped against my husband, who caught me before I rolled off my chair. Popcorn scattered everywhere. "Nurse, help!" Gerry called. "I think my wife has fainted." The lights came on. Mercifully, the film stopped, and the nurse rushed to my aid. I was dizzy and disoriented when I heard her impossible request.

"Put your head between your knees," she commanded.

"I can't!" I slurred. Gerry tried to help, but my advanced pregnancy thwarted our success. Unable to fold me in half, he bent my swollen torso as far forward as possible—about six inches—and steadied me.

When I had been revived, we agreed I had seen enough. I was escorted to the waiting room and laid out on the couch. Gerry asked to watch the end of the film while I recovered. "We stopped just when things were getting exciting," he complained. At that point I knew he would be fine in the delivery room...but I was filled with terror over *my* performance.

໑໑໑

Three weeks later, the big day arrived. I woke up at 5 AM and knew this was it. Labor was a long, slow, and—at first—mildly uncomfortable experience. We arrived at the hospital with plenty of time to spare, and after I got situated, I was told there was still a long wait. Gerry and I had read that walking sometimes sped up the process, so we walked miles on the hospital corridors. Too tired to walk any more, we returned to my room to wait. Some time after midnight, things changed dramatically.

I discovered that what I had thought were labor pains were only little tightenings. The first real contraction took my breath away. After five hours of monstrous contractions of unbelievable intensity, I was finally wheeled into the delivery room and told to push. I tried. Forty minutes brought no success. Exhausted as I was from the long day and the miles of corridor walked, and worn down by pain because of my adamant refusal to take any medication, I was looking at a grim prospect. Just about the time the fetal monitor was signaling that we may have to resort to cesarean section, my obstetrician figured out my problem and said something that changed everything. I was able to deliver the baby naturally and quickly because of his instruction.

Up to that point, each time a contraction had ferociously gripped my body, though I thought I was pushing, I was in fact doing something more akin to clenching my teeth or balling up my fist. I was simply tightening up, trying to survive the bone-shattering pain. I didn't know it, but I was trying to protect myself. When the OB-GYN said, "Connie! Push *through* the pain,"

I finally understood. When the next contraction came, I began to push. The pain increased. The more I pushed, the more painful it became, until I feared I could not bear it. At that point, for the past 40 minutes, I had inadvertently stopped pushing and clenched up. This time, when I got to the point where I feared the pain might rip me asunder, *on faith* I trusted the doctor and pushed harder. I felt the baby move—and the pain, instead of increasing with that final push, peaked and receded. Two more of those mighty pushes, and our beautiful daughter fell into the doctor's hands. And, as women over the centuries have said, the pain is immediately forgotten in the thrill of seeing new life.

∾∾∾

In the same way, mature faith requires that we push through the pain. Instead of clenching our wounded heart, tightening up our defenses, and protecting ourselves from further assault, we face the pain and press ahead.

> Since we also have such a large cloud of witnesses surrounding us, let us lay aside every weight and the sin that so easily ensnares us, and run with endurance the race that lies before us, keeping our eyes on Jesus, the source and perfecter of our faith, who for the joy that lay before Him endured a cross and despised the shame, and has sat down at the right hand of God's throne (Hebrews 12:1-2).

The writer of Hebrews exhorts believers to push through the pain; to "run with endurance." And what is "the sin that so easily ensnares us"? Many scholars believe it is the sin of unbelief—the wanderer's modus operandi! We are to keep our eyes on Jesus, stay connected to the Vine, refuse to fall victim to unbelief, and push through the pain of life. Like birthing mothers, we know that the joy that lies before us will erase the memory of the pain we've endured.

Moving On and Moving Forward in Our Faith

The phrase "born again" so aptly describes our true condition. As spiritual newborns, we are quite helpless. The Holy Spirit, like a mother, takes us by the hand and leads us through those early days of learning to walk, talk, see, and hear a whole new spiritual realm of experience. However, eventually we learn to walk steadily and run; bit by bit God allows us more leash so we experience a new way of relating to Him. We learn to trust Him and, as we do, He trusts us as well. (There we can relate to Mother Teresa's tongue-in-cheek comment: "I know God will not give me anything I can't handle. I just wish that He didn't trust me so much."[3])

As babies, when we cry, our mothers feed us, change us, and rock us, and we learn to expect quick responses to our cries. As young believers, that is often our experience as well. I remember feeling a strong sense of having God speak to my needs and supply me with an abundance of peace and joy. He seemed so close. So attentive. So real! But when life got harder and God did not seem as motherly, I began to wonder where He had gone. What was happening was that God was trying to steer me toward a mature relationship with Him. But I still wanted to be babied. He was trying to get me to stand on the edge of the nest and try my wings. But I wanted to stay huddled in the center, complaining loudly and waiting for nourishment to be dropped into my open beak!

God wants to take us to a new level.

A problem many believers have is that instead of moving on in our faith and allowing our understanding of God to grow and change, we keep going back and pounding on the gates of Eden— wanting to return to those carefree days of spiritual youth when God walked and talked with us and seemed so near, so real. God, meanwhile, wants us to mature and grow and toughen up so we can survive in the real world—which is east of Eden. Eden lasts for only a season. It's what we do outside the garden that determines the depth of relationship with our heavenly Father. God wants to take us to a new level.

Some of us, though, don't trust God because we don't trust anybody. Katya grew up in a home where her mother rejected her and her father was a "nonentity." The one teacher she idolized disappointed her. The father of her children told her when their oldest was in kindergarten that he didn't want the responsibility of a wife and three kids anymore.

Many years passed before she allowed herself to be vulnerable enough to fall in love again. Her second husband, whom she loved and trusted, shattered her heart when, after a year, he revealed he had a wife and a family in another country. He said he had married her only to expedite his request for a work visa. Once again she was betrayed and abandoned. With almost every person in her life who mattered having failed her, it was hard for her to trust God.

"It came to me that what faith is, is giving up control. I learned young that the only way to be safe was to be in control," says Katya, now in her 50s. Even though the latter half of Katya's life has included some close relationships of mutual trust, her early experiences have left their mark. Her relationship with an unseen God has often been a struggle. Periods of deep communion are short-lived and interspersed with seasons of doubt and feelings of abandonment.

❧ ❧ ❧

Afraid of people, afraid of God; afraid to go forward, afraid to let go of the past—not a pretty picture is it? But that is how life looks through the eyes of a wanderer. The road out of the wilderness is walked, hand in hand, with the Father. The recovering wanderer chooses to take His hand, to look ahead, to courageously push through the pain, trusting that his "little faith" will be enough. The recovering wanderer *chooses* to trust.

No, there is no going back, only going forward—to a new place. A better place. A place for those who have a mature faith in the real God.

A Letter from a Friend

I will give you a new heart and
put a new spirit within you;
I will remove your heart of stone
and give you a heart of flesh.
I will place My Spirit within you and cause you
to follow My statutes and carefully observe My ordinances.
Then you will live in the land that I gave your fathers;
you will be My people, and I will be your God.
God speaking through the prophet Ezekiel

This letter from my friend Toni is included with her permission.

DEAR CONNIE

In the darkest days of my struggle, when swirling masses of confusion consumed me, one thing that grieved my heart was that I would never be able to share my experience with anyone—for it was beyond words, beyond comprehension. When you asked to hear my story, I was not at all sure God had brought me to the point of putting my journey into words. The fact that you hear me, understand me, can relate to where I am, is the hugest of blessings to my still-tender heart.

When I come before Him, in that safest place of all, what often pours out of the depths of me is, "God, I am *alone* on this journey; I am *lonely* on this journey. It seems I am going where none has gone before…" It seems, though, that God wants me to know that this road is not so highly unusual, not entirely void of other travelers. He knows how badly I too need, as you so aptly put it, the encouragement of linking souls with a sister in Christ on this same journey.

I told you that when I heard you speak about your own wilderness experience, you could have used my journal to write your talk. Let me clarify—the *end* of your talk came from my journal. My story is actually quite different from yours, but we ended up at the same place—hearing God's call.

I came to the Lord as a child. Never rebelled. Never questioned. Wanted to please God. Sought His will. God blessed me with a wonderful, godly husband. Our life has been free from tragedy or strife, filled with blessing after blessing, especially our six precious children.

I cannot put my finger on when it happened. Somewhere along the way, my passion for God waned. I didn't know it, couldn't see it. I was still busy at church, busy at home, morally upright, and very content. God and I definitely still had a relationship (but then, we know how God feels about lukewarmness, don't we?).

I have a dear, dear friend from college—a special, forever, heart-to-heart friend—named Melissa. She's the friend who will always love me, no matter what. In May 2002, Melissa became pregnant with her first baby, a much-wanted, much-prayed-for child, conceived after a long process of fertility treatments. In October of that year, Melissa lost her baby daughter and nearly died herself.

To this day, I don't know why that event affected me the way it did. I went sliding down a mountainside, right off the edge of a cliff, into a darkness I had never known before. The pain was unbearable. It was as if a portion of Melissa's grief was placed on me. There is neither time nor "ink" enough to tell you the details of that time in my life… but simply to survive those months was by far the hardest thing ever.

In the blackness of grief, God's care was evident to me in one way only: He gave me a friend to walk beside me. I had known Jane for four years since her husband, Joel, came to pastor our church. She was someone I thought a lot of and enjoyed visiting with, but we were not truly friends. I see now that God was saving the gift of our friendship for the time I needed it most.

The day after Melissa's baby died, I was on a bus with a group of ladies from church going to a women's conference. On the return trip, the shock wore off; the grief descended, and I hit bottom. Jane was my seatmate. Though we had never shared deeply, I knew I couldn't survive alone, so I reached out for her. We rode for hours in the dark with me clinging to her hand in utter despair.

That was the first of many times I turned to Jane in pain, confusion, desperation, and despondency. She never had any more of a clue than I did about what was happening to me or what to do about it, but she held my hand, hugged me, listened to me, and prayed for me.

C.S. Lewis said that pain is God's megaphone. I must agree. Others have said that grief opens us up like surgery so God can do a work deep within. Again, I must agree. It was as if God said to me, "Since you are ripped open, let's clean you out and rearrange you—*totally.*"

Oh, ouch.

He started a process that continues even now. He took me *way* back to square one, and we started completely over. It has been so hard, learning many, many, many lessons. I went to Pastor Joel over and over with deep theological questions and to Jane with deep heart questions (and to my husband, Mike, with both).

God had me in His Word five or six hours a day. I read it cover to cover in three months. Then I read it again... so much glorious revelation in the midst of continued struggle. But I fell in love with Him like I didn't know I could. He didn't leave me in the muddy pit of grief, and He didn't leave me without help. Jane and Pastor Joel (and Mike) alone knew my struggles. I so appreciated them and depended on their love and support and strength. I thanked God for them constantly.

Then—*bombshell*—Jane and Joel moved away to California. Once again, blackness descended.

Crushed to fine powder is the best description I can give of myself at that point. This time there were no humans to be God's hands to me. I had my dear husband, and he tried his best—but I knew, of course, he was not sufficient. I cried out to God like I never had before. In the 11 months since Melissa's baby's death, I had come to know Him as my Rescuer, my Deliverer, the One who is mighty to save, the One worth trusting when nothing makes sense. And *He came. He stayed.* He has been *more* than sufficient. It has not been easy...still is not easy. Jane left 16 months ago, and I still miss her deeply every day. God continues to perform surgery, and it often hurts.

Oh, but I wouldn't trade the pain of the past two-and-a-half years for anything. He has taught me enough *truth* to fill volumes. (Here's the part where I thought you borrowed my journal.) He gave me Luke 22:32 early on ("When you have returned to Me, strengthen your brethren"). I remember taking it to Pastor Joel and asking what it might mean, because God took me back to that verse over and over.

Later, He gave me Psalm 51:6 and 12 and 13 ("You desire truth in the inward parts...Restore to me the joy of your salvation...Then I will teach transgressors Your ways..."). The page from my journal I wanted to send you was the day I caught on to what He meant by those verses and how they were connected. I basically wrote, "When will I teach transgressors? Oh, I see—when I have returned! When He has restored me, then I will be able to strengthen others."

One truth I'd like to shout from the mountaintops is, *God gives beauty for ashes.* Melissa and her husband just celebrated the one-year anniversary of the adoption of their three daughters from China, now ages six, three, and one. And they have moved to my state, so after nine years of being separated by thousands of miles, we actually get to see each other on occasion.

Pastor Joel and Jane continue to be dear friends. They had some difficult times several months after their move, and it happened just like Jesus said it would: I had the privilege of strengthening Jane and being there for her, just as she had been there for me.

As for me, I am a *different person* than I was two years ago. He removed my heart of stone and gave me a heart of flesh. He has taught me to abide in the Vine, and fruit is popping out all over. I know firsthand God's power to transform. He has filled me with *hope.* I've seen His hope come to shine in others' eyes because He allows me to love and serve them and teach them what He has taught me.

I stopped asking Him a long time ago when this still-difficult "let's-change-Toni" process will end. I'm beginning to realize He doesn't intend for it to end...And I think I'm glad...

You are the first I've shared my story with. Thank you for listening.

TONI

Acknowledgments

*I*f you are reading these pages you are either looking for your name or, like me, you don't feel you've gotten your money's worth unless you've read every word printed. Either way, I hope you're not disappointed by what you find.

There aren't enough words to say how much I owe to Karen Willoughby, my friend, my writing coach, my e-pal. She spent thousands of hours teaching me basic journalism via e-mail in her "spare" time. She helped sell my first magazine story in 1997 and encouraged me from the beginning to pursue my dream of authorship. Anything good in my writing, I attribute to her tutelage.

But even before Karen, Nancy McGough, editor of the *Baptist Horizon*, gave me my first chance. She taught me to sift through pages of scribbled interview notes and find the quotable gems. Then she published those first pitiful attempts and encouraged me to stick with it.

Thanks to Carolyn Curtis, former editor of *OnMission* magazine (and friend), who published hundreds of my articles and never wavered in her belief that I would author a book.

To those poor souls who slogged through early drafts of this manuscript and still call me friend, I am hugely grateful: Kathy Howard, Marie-Louise Ternier-Gommers, and Frank Stirk. Each of them busy with their own writing, they gave me the precious gift of time, and their feedback altered my course more than once.

Thanks to Paul Gossard, my editor at Harvest House who, like a master quilter, moved the squares around—tossed out a few that didn't quite fit—and helped me stitch together the remainder into something I could be proud to display in public.

To Cindy Buntain, Susan Booth, and Kathy Howard—you prove that loyal friendship endures, cannot be earned, and can never be repaid.

To my five sisters, near and far, who laugh at my stories and ask for more—thank you for believing I could write a "serious" book and convincing me to try. To my brother, whose "writer's retreat on wheels" in Waterton Park helped me get moving on this project, thank you.

And to the "pray-er" who lives on the other side of the Blue Glass, lifting me up daily—sometimes hourly—to the One who enables, empowers, and equips, I am indebted beyond measure. Her fervent intercession (and more than one pot of homemade soup!) strengthened me so I could run with endurance and finish the race.

Finally, to the living God who did not leave me in the barren wilderness, I offer up this manuscript, hoping it is a sweet aroma and pleasing in Your sight.

Please note, although the stories in this book are true, in some cases I have changed names and details to protect confidentiality.

About the Author

A recognized evangelical writer and speaker, **Connie Cavanaugh** is a featured columnist for *HomeLife* magazine and a regular contributor to *OnMission* magazine. She speaks extensively at conferences and retreats. She lives in Alberta, Canada, with her husband, Gerry.

To view live video and audio clips that illustrate Connie's dynamic speaking style, visit her on the Web at www.conniecavanaugh.com. Follow the links to see her calendar, to check out retreat and seminar topics, or to contact her directly with booking queries, comments, or questions related to her ministry.

You can also reach Connie by writing or e-mailing her:

Connie Cavanaugh
100 Convention Way
Cochrane, AB T4C 2G2
ccav@ccsb.ca

Notes

Chapter 2—Spiritual Drift

1. Larry Crabb, *Shattered Dreams* (Colorado Springs, CO: WaterBrook Press, 2001), pp. 185, 21.

2. C.S. Lewis, *The Four Loves* (New York: Harcourt, Brace and Company, 1960), p. 169.

3. Lewis.

4. Ray C. Stedman, *Authentic Christianity* (Grand Rapids, MI: Discovery House Publishers, 1996), p. 18.

5. Stedman, p. 17.

Chapter 4—Thou Shalt Have No Other Gods

1. Lynne Hybels's story is on a compact disk recording of a talk she gave to pastors and wives in Ottawa, Ontario, Canada, in 2003. Used by permission.

2. Carol Kent, *Tame Your Fears* (Colorado Springs, CO: Navpress, 2003), p. 173.

Chapter 5—The God Who Pursues

1. John R.W. Stott, *Authentic Christianity* (Downer's Grove, IL: InterVarsity Press, 1995), p. 17.

2. From an article in Loretta Ross, *Making Haqqodesh* (a quarterly newsletter published by The Sanctuary, Topeka, Kansas), vol. 15, no. 4, "Lent and Eastertide," 2004, p. 2.

3. Gary Thomas, "Winter of the Soul," *Homelife* magazine, May 2004, pp. 48-51.

4. Henry Blackaby and Claude King, *Experiencing God* (Nashville, TN: Broadman & Holman, 1994), p. 36.

Chapter 6—Undying Love

1. Eugene Peterson, *The Message* (Colorado Springs, CO: NavPress Publishing Group, 2002), p. 1608.

2. Mark Buchanan, *Your God Is Too Safe* (Sisters, OR: Multnomah Publishers, Inc., 2001), p. 109.

Chapter 7—Come Out with Your Hands Up

1. Rick Warren, *The Purpose-Driven Life* (Grand Rapids, MI: Zondervan, 2002), pp. 81-84.

2. John Ortberg, *If You Want to Walk on Water, You've Got to Get Out of the Boat* (Grand Rapids, MI: Zondervan, 2001), p. 69.

Chapter 8—Break the Conspiracy of Silence

1. Ray C. Stedman, *Authentic Christianity* (Grand Rapids, MI: Discovery House Publishers, 1996), p. 17.

2. As quoted in Stedman, p. 18.

3. Clarence H. Snyder, "The Steps of A.A.—An Interpretation," January 1972. Snyder started the first AA group in Cleveland, Ohio, on May 18, 1939. He is a member of the founding Oxford Alcoholics Anonymous group. Read his story at www.barefoots world.net/clarence.

Chapter 9—Reckless Obedience

1. Oswald Chambers, *My Utmost for His Highest,* updated ed. (Grand Rapids, MI: Discovery House Publishers, 1992), June 18.

2. John Eldredge, *Waking the Dead* (Nashville, TN: Thomas Nelson Publishers, 2003), p. 102.

3. Eldredge, p. 95.

4. John Ortberg, *If You Want to Walk on Water, You've Got to Get Out of the Boat* (Grand Rapids, MI: Zondervan, 1995), p. 15.

5. Ortberg, p. 17.

6. Ortberg, p. 17.

7. Philip Yancey, *The Jesus I Never Knew* (Grand Rapids, MI: Zondervan, 1995), p. 80.

8. Henry T. Blackaby, message given at Bow Valley Baptist Church, Cochrane, Alberta, 2004.

Chapter 10—Full of Grace

1. Philip Yancey, *What's So Amazing About Grace?* (Grand Rapids, MI: Zondervan Publishing House, 1997), p. 70.

2. Brennan Manning, *The Ragamuffin Gospel* (Sisters, OR: Multnomah Publishers, Inc., 1990), p. 14.

3. Charles R. Swindoll, *The Grace Awakening* (Dallas, TX: Word Publishing, 1996).

4. From the hymn "Amazing Grace! How Sweet the Sound," words by John Newton (1725–1807).

Chapter 11—Sweat Equity

1. Habitat for Humanity Web site: www.habitat.org.

2. Walter W. Skeat, *The Concise Dictionary of English Etymology* (Cumberland House, Hertfordshire: Wordsworth Editions Ltd., 1993), p. 119.

3. Mark Buchanan, *Your God Is Too Safe* (Sisters, OR: Multnomah Publishers, 2001), p. 130.

4. Bill Hybels, *Honest to God* (Grand Rapids, MI: Zondervan, 1990), p. 11.

5. Rick Warren, *The Purpose-Driven Life* (Grand Rapids, MI: Zondervan, 2002), p. 75.

6. John Eldredge, *Waking the Dead* (Nashville, TN: Thomas Nelson Publishers, 2003), p. 210.

Chapter 12—Unmasking

1. Kevin Cavanaugh, Senior Pastor, Cedar Grove Baptist Church, Surrey, British Columbia, "Weathering the Storms and Seasons of Marriage" Seminar, June 28, 2004.

Chapter 13—There's Only One You

1. Henry Blackaby and Claude King, *Experiencing God* (Nashville, TN: Broadman & Holman, 1994), p. 170.

2. Rick Warren, *The Purpose-Driven Life* (Grand Rapids, MI: Zondervan, 2002), p. 241.

3. Warren, p. 241.

4. Walter Brueggemann, *Finally Comes the Poet: Daring Speech for Proclamation*, (Minneapolis, MN: Fortress, 1989), as quoted by Warren Wiersbe, *Preaching and Teaching with Imagination* (Wheaton, IL: Victor Books/SP Publications, 1994), p. 64.

5. Chuck Colson as quoted by John Ortberg, *If You Want to Walk on Water, You've Got to Get Out of the Boat* (Grand Rapids, MI: Zondervan, 2001), p. 72.

6. David Roper, *Jacob: The Fools God Chooses* (Grand Rapids, MI: Discovery House Publishers, 2002), p. 39, emphasis added.

7. Larry Crabb, *Shattered Dreams* (Colorado Springs, CO: WaterBrook Press, 2001) p. 73.

Chapter 14—The Personal God

1. Interview with Kirk and Laura Boes, Whistler, British Columbia, August 2002.

2. Mark Buchanan, *Your God Is Too Safe* (Sisters, OR: Multnomah Publishers, Inc., 2001), p. 139.

3. Beth Moore, *The Beloved Disciple* (Nashville, TN: Broadman & Holman Publishers, 2003), pp. 132-133.

4. From an article in Loretta Ross, *Making Haqqodesh* (a quarterly newsletter published by The Sanctuary, Topeka, Kansas), vol. 15, no. 4, "Lent and Eastertide," 2004, p. 1.

5. John Eldredge, *Waking the Dead* (Nashville, TN: Thomas Nelson Publishers, 2003), p. 13.

6. Jeff Christopherson, Senior Pastor of The Sanctuary Church Planting Community in Oakville, Ontario, Canada. Message given during the Fall Revival at the Canadian Southern Baptist Seminary, September 2004.

Chapter 15—In Whom We Trust

1. Jerry Bridges, *The Joy of Fearing God* (Colorado Springs, CO: Waterbrook Press, 1997).

2. Craig L. Blomberg, *Jesus and the Gospels* (Nashville, TN: Broadman & Holman Publishers, 1997), p. 164. Blomberg is commenting on Robert Kysar, *John: The Maverick Gospel* (Atlanta, GA: John Knox Publishers, 1976), pp. 67-73.

3. Mother Teresa, as quoted on www.mysticcowboy.org/archives/000587.html.

Other Good ——— Harvest House Reading

Becoming Who God Intended
by David Eckman

Whether you realize it or not, your imagination is filled with *pictures* of reality. The Bible indicates these pictures reveal your true "heart beliefs"—the beliefs that actually shape your everyday feelings and reactions to family, friends, and others, to life's circumstances, and to God.

David Eckman compassionately shows you how to allow God's Spirit to build new, *biblical* pictures in your heart and imagination. As you do this, you will be able to accept God's acceptance of you in Christ, break free of negative emotions and habitual sin...and finally experience the life God the Father has always intended for you.

> "David Eckman is a man you can trust...
> His teaching resonates with God's wisdom and compassion."
> —**Stu Weber**, author of *Tender Warrior* and
> *Four Pillars of a Man's Heart*

ન્જ ન્જ ન્જ

Grace Amazing
by Steve McVey

If your Christian life seems as dry as dust and you're just going around in circles...*maybe you're wandering in the wilderness.*
  In the wilderness, you feel as though...

- you live by the rules, and the Bible is the rule book

- you work hard for God...but you never quite measure up

In the land of God's amazing grace, you experience the truth that...

- God has made you alive *in Christ*—and now you want to do what He wants

- Jesus has done all the work, and you can rest in the Father's acceptance

Steve McVey reveals to you more of the heart of your loving, giving Father...so you can better grasp just why His grace is so amazing.

HARVEST HOUSE
PUBLISHERS